MODERN SOVIET ARMOR

MODERN SOVIET ARMOR

ARMOR

Combat Vehicles of the USSR and Warsaw Pact Today
Steven J. Zaloga

Prentice-Hall, Inc.,
Englewood Cliffs, N.J.

Glossary

Abbreviation	Full term	Description
AA	Anti-aircraft	
AP	Armour Piercing	
APDS	Armour Piercing, Discarding Sabot	A type of anti-tank ammunition using a sub-calibre penetrator encased in a sabot, which separates from the penetrator once the projectile has left the gun barrel
APHE	Armour Piercing High Explosive	An anti-tank projectile with explosive filler
AT	Anti-tank	
BMD	Bronevaya Maschina Desantnaya	Airborne combat vehicle
BMP	Bronevaya Maschina Piekhota	Infantry combat vehicle
BMP-SON	Bronevaya Maschina Piekhota-Stantsiya Orudiynoy Navodki	Infantry combat vehicle-fire control radar
BRDM	Bronirovannaya Razviedyvatielno Dozornaja Maschina	Armoured scout vehicle
BRT	BroneTransportR	Armoured transporter
BWP	Bojowy Woz Piechoty	Polish infantry combat vehicle
DP		Soviet designation for a radiation detector. (Not to be confused with the other DP acronym 'Degtyarev-piekhota', which was a Second World War Soviet squad machine-gun
FNLA	Frente Nacional Libertação de Angola	National Front for the Liberation of Angola
Frag-HE	Fragmentation-High Explosive	An artillery round that, on explosion of the filler, sprays shrapnel
FUG	Felderito Uszo Gepkosci	Hungarian amphibious scout car
GAZ	Gorkii Avtomobil Zavod	Automotive factory in Gorkii
GSP	Gusenichnii Samokhodnii Parom	Tracked ferry vehicle
HE	High Explosive	
HEAT	High Explosive, Anti-Tank	An anti-tank projectile using a shaped charge, explosive warhead to penetrate the armour, rather than a kinetic penetrator as in the case of AP and APHE rounds; also called HESH (High Explosive, Shaped Head)
HVAP	High Velocity Armour Piercing	An anti-tank projectile, usually an APDS or the related APFSDS (Armour Piercing Fin-Stabilized Discarding Sabot) type
IR	Infra-red	
JOW	Jednostki Obrony Wybrzeza	Polish coastal defence unit
LAW	Light Anti-Tank Weapon	
NATO	North Atlantic Treaty Organization	
NBC	Nuclear, Biological, Chemical Warfare	Also called CBR (Chemical, Biological, Radiological) or ABC (Atomic, Biological, Chemical)
OPVT		Underwater tank snorkel
PAZ		Contaminant protection system
PTG	Plywajacy Transporter Gasienicowy	Polish amphibious tracked transporter
PUAZO		Anti-aircraft fire control director
PVO	Protivovozdushnaya Oborona	Soviet Air Defence units
SV	Sukhoputnyk Voisk	Soviet Ground Forces
TOW	Tube-launched, Optically-tracked, Wire-guided	A heavy assault ground-to-ground (or air-to-ground) anti-tank guided weapon system
UNITA	Uniao Nacional para a Independencia Total de Angola	National Union for the Total Independence of Angola
VDV	Vozdushno Desantniye Voiska	Soviet Airborne Forces
VVS	Voyenno Vozdushnyye Sily	Soviet Air Force
WAT	Wojskowa Akademia Techniczna	Polish Military Technical Academy
WPT	Woz Pogotowia Technicznego	Polish technical repair vehicle
ZIS	Zavod imeni Stalina	Moscow-based factory named after Stalin
ZSU	Zenitny Samochodnaya Ustanovka	Self-propelled anti-aircraft mount

Contents

First American edition
published by
Prentice-Hall, 1979
Reprinted 1980

ISBN 0-13597-856-4
Library of Congress Catalog Card Number 79-84836

To my youngest brother, Danny.

Edited by Tessa Rose.
Designed by Anthony A. Evans.
Typeset by Trade Linotype, Birmingham.
Printed in Great Britain by Morrison & Gibb Ltd, Edinburgh.

Preface

The Soviet Ground Forces (Sukhoputnykh Voisk) are centred around mechanized units, which are in turn dependent upon tracked and wheeled combat vehicles. To understand the capabilities and limitations of these Ground Forces, it is important to understand the capabilities of the equipment on which the Soviet Army depends. This book attempts to do more than catalogue the current Soviet arsenal. But, rather than devote inordinate attention to each and every vehicle sub-type, no matter how minor, we have placed the emphasis on the major vehicle types, and have paid special attention to the newer generations of equipment that will serve with the Ground Forces in the 1980s. Besides Soviet manufactured vehicles, where relevant there is also coverage on derivative types built by the Warsaw Pact countries and China.

A note should be made here regarding vehicle designations presented in this book. In the case of a large proportion of the more recent vehicle types, and some of the older types, the true Soviet designation is not known. Consequently, NATO has adopted a standardized system of code-names to label unidentified new weapons. These names will be most evident when referring to radar, surface-to-air missiles and wire guided anti-tank missiles. The Soviet Army is rather miserly in allotting vehicle sub-type designations: for example, they do not distinguish an early production T-54 tank with the wide mantlet and many other outdated features from a late production machine with the standard turret, infra-red gear, refitted NBC filtration system and a host of other improvements. Because of this, many NATO armies have developed their own designation systems for the major sub-types. This is all well and good, except that there is no standardized method of allotting these designations. As a result, the vehicle type designated T-55A by the US Army is called T-55C by the West German Army. The designations used in this book are based on the US Army designations, or commonly accepted standardized NATO designations. However, when known, the Soviet designations have been used in preference to all others.

This matter is further complicated by the fact that the Warsaw Pact countries rename vehicles when they enter their service; for example, the Soviet K-61 amphibian tractor is called the PTG when used in Polish service. Again, in this case, preference has been given to the Soviet designation, though common Warsaw Pact designations have often been mentioned.

The reader's indulgence is begged for the quality of some of the photographs. In the case of many support vehicles, there are few, if any, good unclassified photographs, and we have been obliged to use rather poor copies when they were the only illustrations available.

All data is provided in both imperial and metric weight or measure. The only exception to this rule is 'tons', which are presented in metric only.

The scale plans included are all to a constant 1/76 scale.

The author owes a great debt of gratitude to a score of people for their assistance on this project—above all, to James W. Loop. Thanks go to Karl Rosenlof, Kalevi Moilanen, George Balin, Joseph Desautels, Esa Muikku, Charles Kliment, Charles Perkins and Lt. Col. Robert Icks, for their generous help in providing photographs from their personal collections; to Mrs. Vika Edwards and Robin Roseman who good-naturedly put up with frequent rummaging through the files of the Sovfoto bureau in New York; to Major Patrick Cannan of the US Army Public Information Office and Dana Bell of the US Air Force photographic archives for their aid in obtaining some of the photographs; to Lee Ness for the loan of a considerable quantity of material on Soviet Ground Forces organization; to Jack Zaloga, who spent many an hour in the darkroom preparing photographs. We would also like to thank several friends serving in the US Armed Forces. Thanks also to various friends in Eastern Europe, whose names are better left unmentioned. And last but not least, to Stephanie, without whose patient encouragement during a dark time this book never would have been started.

Steven J. Zaloga, 1979

Below: In the past decade, the Soviet Union has markedly stepped up its export of military equipment to Third World countries. This has been most noticeable in the civil wars and other conflicts in Sub-Saharan Africa. These T-55s parading in Luanda in 1976 belong to the 1st Angolan Armoured Regiment. The massive injection of Soviet arms into the civil war, coupled with the provisioning of Cuban troops, threw the balance in favour of the FNLA forces over their UNITA rivals. T-55s arrived rather late in the conflict, and older T-34/85s bore the brunt of the action. Although these T-55s are equipped with infra-red sights, they do not have the main L-2G searchlight fitted to the right of the main gun. (Sovfoto)

Battle Tanks

The key weapon in the arsenal of the Soviet Ground Forces is the tank. And the central role played by armoured units in gaining the Soviets victory during the Second World War has ensured continued interest in tank development by the Soviet Union's military and political élites in the post-war years. Nevertheless, Soviet military leaders have not underestimated the serious shortcomings of the wartime Red Army and have made strenuous efforts to close the gap with the formerly more sophisticated armies of Western Europe. Wartime production priorities forced Soviet automotive works and other branches in the heavy industries field to concentrate solely on tanks and self-propelled guns to the near exclusion of troop carriers, trucks and tracked support vehicles, and this led to a very low level of mechanization. The avaricious demands of mechanized units for wheeled and tracked support vehicles was provided largely through Lend-Lease equipment and the pre-war automotive and tractor pool. In contrast to the wartime situation, Soviet industry now provides the Army with a broad range of mechanized equipment.

The T-34

The single most influential factor in affecting contemporary Soviet tank design philosophy was the unparalleled success of the T-34 medium tank during the Second World War. This vehicle proved to possess the three indispensible virtues of a good design: firepower, mobility and armoured protection. The same could be said for many of its opponents, such as the superlative German Panther, but what singled out the T-34 (and, for that matter, its American counterpart, the Sherman), was its reliability in the field, its low unit cost and its ease of manufacture. It proved to be a simple, robust vehicle, requiring a minimum of daily maintenance, and well suited to the average, mechanically naïve Russian tank crew. The T-34 was designed with a ruthless no-frills philosophy that left it with a very rough-edged finish but without compromising any of its key performance requirements. Armour welding on the T-34 appalled German craftsmen, but was, in fact, not so

poor as to reduce the protective characteristics of the armour. Exterior machining was frequently crude, except at key joints and interfaces where it was quite good.

The T-34 was certainly a fatiguing and uncomfortable vehicle to crew, and was marginally inferior to some German types in the later years of the war. But the simplicity of its design allowed it to be produced in quantities two- or three-fold over its complicated and expensive German opponents. Although the German Panther was a technically brilliant design that could easily smother a T-34 on a one-to-one basis, unfortunately for the Wehrmacht, it was nearly twice as heavy as the T-34, cost two or three times as much to produce, and was infinitely more complicated and expensive to transport, repair, fuel and maintain. As a result, the single Panther was swamped by an unequal number of T-34s, which, while not displaying the German tank's well-machined finesse, were perfectly adequate for their task.

Soviet logistics were often so marginal that the large pool of T-34s proved a real blessing. Whereas German units were obliged to go to considerable trouble and expense retrieving their costly broken-down tanks, Russian formations expended their tanks and were replaced by freshly-equipped units.

The shortcomings of the T-34 became more apparent as the war dragged on, but Soviet leaders, unlike their German counterparts, were unwilling to interrupt the steady flow of tanks from the Ural tank works in favour of a new, marginally improved type. So, it was not until 1944, with the conclusion of the war inevitable, that the T-34's successor was slowly introduced onto the assembly lines. The T-34 remained in production in the Soviet Union until the late 1940s, and was produced later in Czechoslovakia and Poland well into the 1950s. Its last significant variant, the T-34-85, which entered service in 1944, was widely supplied to the Soviet Union's allies, and saw considerable action in the fighting in Korea in 1950, in Hungary (on both sides) in 1956, in Sinai in 1956, on the Syrian front in 1967 and 1973, Vietnam in 1972-73, and in a dozen other wars

Below: In the late 1960s, many old mothballed T-34-85s were re-manufactured and exported. These T-34-85s belong to the North Vietnamese Army. This photograph was taken in 1972, before the famous Easter offensive. Although a few T-34-85s were encountered south of the Demilitarized Zone, most were kept in the North for training. The re-manufactured T-34-85s can easily be distinguished by their new T-55-style wheels and other additions, such as night driving lights. Many were also fitted with uprated engines. The North Vietnamese Army insignia consists of a yellow star and circle over a red disc; the numbers on the turrets are painted in white. (Sovfoto)

Left: The Chinese Army received many T-34-85s from the Soviet Union before the onset of the current antagonism between the two countries. Some of these were converted for anti-aircraft duty, and are known as the Type 63. The conversion was quite crude and consisted of a twin Type 55 37mm gun in a thinly armoured turret with external stowage panniers added. This particular vehicle was captured from the North Vietnamese and still displays their markings. The yellow star with red disc insignia was seldom seen on North Vietnamese tanks operating in South Vietnam.

Left: The T-44 first entered production in 1944. These T-44Ms were still working in a Category III tank battalion in 1973. The vehicle in the foreground is fitted with a KMT-4 mine plough and a bulldozer blade. The T-44 could be fitted with either the old V-shaped STU plough, or the newer BTU plough. The vision slit in front of the driver's position was peculiar to the T-44. Otherwise, the T-44 hull was very similar to that on the T-54. (Sovfoto)

both major and minor, most recently with Cuban troops in Angola. By the late 1960s the T-34 had been withdrawn from most Soviet units, where it had been labouring on for training purposes; in the event of a war some still might be called up for Category III units.

After the war, numerous minor improvements were made on the T-34-85 and, as late as the 1960s, many old hulks were re-manufactured, using the wheels and engine components from T-54s. Many T-34s were fitted with snorkelling equipment for crossing shallow rivers, and even when many were finally withdrawn as gun tanks, their chassis were rebuilt as armoured recovery vehicles. The Czech version was easily distinguishable from the Russian-built machines by its different turret casting. Many of these were sold to the Egyptian Army and saw service in the various Middle East conflicts. The Polish-made T-34-85s closely resembled the Soviet models, but had a number of mechanical improvements. The two improved variants were designated T-34-85 M-1 and T-34-85 M-2. Production there ceased in 1956.

Though the T-34 no longer serves as a battle tank in the Soviet Army, some quantity probably remain in mothballs in case of an emergency or for export, while others are being expended as range targets. Similarly, most of the Warsaw Pact armies have withdrawn their T-34s, limiting their use to a training role or as war reserves. The T-34-85 remains on active duty in several Third World countries and probably in China. Hardly a bad record for a tank nearly forty years old!

The T-44

The T-34's successor was the closely related T-44. This tank represented a drastically modernized T-34-85, and entered production in 1944. The most notable change between the two types was in the hull area. The turret was very similar to that on the T-34-85, but was longer at the rear, had only a single roof vent and, due to the removal of the thick turret collar ring, lacked the T-34-85's goose-necked appearance. Running gear on the early models was identical to that on the T-34, except that the Christie spring suspension was dropped in favour of a conventional torsion bar arrangement. The hull was lower and sleeker than that on the T-34. But a price had to be paid for these changes. Internal space in the T-44 was far more limited than in the already cramped T-34. The power plant, a close derivative of the T-34's V-2, was crammed laterally at the extreme end of the vehicle along with a new transmission. This left very little room in the hull, forcing the Morozov design team to drop the crew complement from five to four. Some of the fuel had to be stored externally, which was hardly ideal. Another fuel cell was located around the ammunition rack to the right of the driver under the glacis plate, which would subsequently prove to be an Achilles' heel in combat.

Nevertheless, in spite of these design compromises, the T-44 was a compact, inexpensive and potent new design, much in the T-34 tradition. It would serve as the basis for nearly thirty years of Soviet tank development. Though much maligned in the Western military press due to

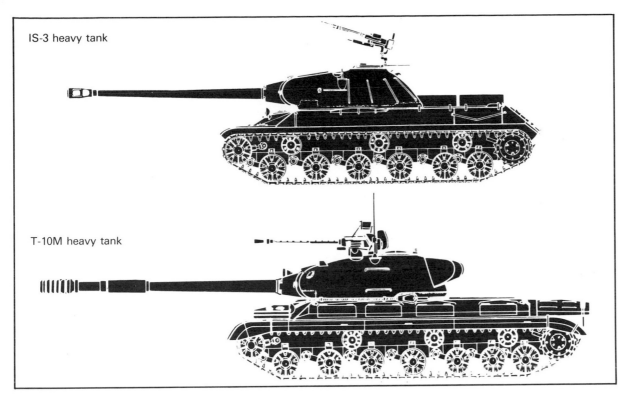

IS-3 heavy tank

T-10M heavy tank

supposed early teething problems with the transmission, it was well received by the Red Army and continues to serve in dwindling numbers with some Category III units.

The main deficiency of the T-44 was the limited development potential of its turret, which was a leftover from the T-34. Attempts were made to rearm both types with the D-10T 100mm gun, but these efforts were not successful and no series production was undertaken. The T-44 prototype fitted with the D-10 had a modified turret with a large bulge on the left turret side to better accommodate the gun. Later production T-44s, designated T-44M, were fitted with a new narrow pitch track, a more conventional drive sprocket arrangement and other modifications that would eventually be standardized in the subsequent T-54 series.

The IS-2, IS-3 and T-10
Though the T-34 was the standard medium tank of the Red Army during the Second World War, it was complemented by a number of heavy tank types. In 1944 it fought alongside the excellent IS-2 Stalin heavy tank for the first time, and the following year the IS-3 Pike was introduced. Both of these tanks were parallel designs of the Dukhov SKB-2 design bureau at Chelyabinsk, although they were prepared by separate teams. The IS-2 was heavily based on the previous KV heavy tank series, especially the experimental KV-13. The IS-3 was the more revolutionary of the two designs and caused many a raised eyebrow when first publicly displayed in Berlin in the autumn of 1945. Both types were equipped with a 122mm gun and shared closely related chassis, power plants and transmissions. A third type, the IS-4, with an even more revolutionary oscillating turret, was ready for production at the same time, but was held back due to its complexity. It was eventually produced after the war in very small numbers. As the war drew to a close, the percentage of heavy tanks in the Red Army's arsenal continued to grow at the expense of medium tanks, but, due to various factors, this trend died out in the post-war years.

Production of the IS-2 and the IS-3 continued into the late 1940s, and later variants included the IS-2M and the IS-3M, which incorporated the improved V-54 engine of the T-54 medium tank and had other mechanical modifications. Parallel development of the IS-2 and IS-3 continued in the form of the experimental IS-6, IS-7, IS-8 and IS-9. These prototypes tested out new armour arrangements, power plants and suspensions, finally leading to the IS-10, which entered service in 1958 as the T-10 heavy tank. (The name change was effected due to Khruschev's de-Stalinization programme.) Although the

T-10 took advantage of the mechanical innovations tested during the experimental programme, it was basically a lengthened and modernized IS-3M. It supplemented the IS-3 in Soviet Army heavy tank battalions, and was followed by an improved type, the T-10M. However, neither was numerically significant.

The T-54 and T-55

In spite of the distinct trend in favour of heavy tanks in 1945, none materialized. In 1947, the Morozov team succeeded in mating the D-10 with the T-44 hull, resulting in the new T-54 medium. The D-10T had comparable or better performance than the D-25T of the IS-3M and could defeat any existing foreign tank. Ironically, in 1943 there had been plans to adopt the D-10T on heavy tanks such as the IS-2, but the programme was shelved due to the production advantages of adopting the 122mm gun. Therefore, unlike the situation in 1944-45, when the heavy tanks were needed to supplement the T-34 in dealing with German heavy tanks such as the Royal Tiger, by the 1950s, medium tanks of the new T-54 type could single-handedly hold their own on the battlefield. The T-10M's only advantage over the T-54 was its heavier armour. The IS-3 was placed in reserve in the 1960s and was followed by the T-10 in the 1970s. Heavy tanks are no longer standard equipment of Soviet armoured divisions though some probably still serve with Category III units or for training. There have been unconfirmed reports that the Soviet Union is working on a new heavy tank design, but at the moment, Soviet tank units are based solely around medium tanks, or as they are more popularly called these days, main battle tanks.

After the failure of the up-gunned T-44 project, the Morozov bureau turned to working on an enlarged turret in which to fit the D-10T 100mm gun. By adding armoured fillets at the mid-section of the T-44 hull, they were able to expand the turret ring diameter sufficiently to accommodate the larger weapon. This new turret vaguely resembled the upside-down skillet shape of the IS-3 Pike turret, but was smaller. When the new turret and gun assembly were fitted to a modified T-44M hull, the resulting vehicle was designated T-54. The T-54 entered active service in 1949 and at the time was the most advanced tank of its class in the world.

The first model T-54 shared the same wide mantlet as the preceding T-44, and the numerous overhangs and shot-traps resulted in the turret shape being far from ideal. Consequently, the initial production model was soon followed by an improved type. This second model featured a new 'pig snout' mantlet, but it still had a turret overhang at the rear. It was not until the third model was introduced in the mid-1950s that the now familiar, standard T-54 emerged. The third model retained the 'pig snout' mantlet, but dispensed with the turret overhang. This new turret resembled a horseshoe crab shell and consisted of three major pieces: the turret casting proper, and two flat roof panels out of which sprouted the loader's and tank commander's hatches. After the termination of T-34 production in Czechoslovakia and Poland, both countries started producing T-54s. Poland began manufacture in 1956.

The T-54 is a straightforward, conventional design, noteworthy for its small size in comparison to comparable Western European or American designs. It has a four-man crew, consisting of a driver, gunner, gun loader and commander. It has good speed and manoeuvrability, though its loose 'dead' track is more apt to shed during violent turns than the track types used on Western tanks. Its 100mm gun is comparable to the 90mm gun used on the American M-48 Patton.

The hull is of a conventional welded construction with a simple box-like cross-section and boat-hull flanged edges where the suspension arms meet the hull. The transmission and engine are located at the rear of the hull, and, unlike conventional designs, the engine is mounted transversely against the axis of travel. Engine fuel is stored internally in two cells; one beside the driver around the ammunition under the right side of the glacis plate, and another just before the engine. This internal fuel capacity of 115 gallons (522 litres) is supplemented by three external fuel panniers of 21 gallons (95 litres) each. Depending upon the production batch, T-54s can also be fitted with either one

Left, top: This T-54 was from the initial production batch. It is fitted with a wide mantlet, and has a rounded turret casting with distinct undercuts at both front and rear. This particular vehicle is fitted with a BTU bulldozer blade.

Left, centre: This T-54, serving with a motorized rifle division in the Siberian Military District in 1976 is of the second production batch. While it has the distinctive 'pig snout' mantlet of later, standard production T-54s, it has a noticeable turret overhang at the rear. It is fitted with the early, unstabilized D-10T gun. In this particular operation, it is supporting an infantry assault with BMPs evident in the background. (Sovfoto)

Left, bottom: The T-54(M) was a late production T-54 or retrofitted T-54 with new features, such as infra-red searchlights and sights and single-plane gun stabilization. This T-54(M) shows the distinctive features of this model. The stabilizer fitted to the new D-10TG gun had to be counterbalanced, and initially a counterweight was fitted (as on this vehicle) to the end of the gun barrel. Subsequently, the D-10TG was fitted with a bore evacuator, which counterbalanced the gun without the weight. On this vehicle, the Dushka anti-aircraft machine-gun has been removed from its mount over the loader's hatch on the right of the turret and stored in a canvas sleeve on racks at the turret rear. (Sovfoto)

or two additional 44-gallon drums (200 litres) at the rear of the hull, bringing the total to approximately 264 gallons (1,200 litres). Beneath the large fuel drums, or to the side, the older models could carry two BDSh smoke dispensers, but retrofitted models carry the newer thermal smoke discharge system. Most Soviet tanks also carry an unditching beam at the rear.

The driver steers the vehicle using a conventional clutch and brake system. Foreign engineers who have test driven the T-54 have commented on the strength required to drive it. This is due to the absence of pneumatic or hydraulic boosting on the controls although newer Polish- and Czechoslovak-produced machines have this feature. To the right of the driver is a fuel cell and one of the main ammunition racks for the gun. A semi-fixed SGMT 7.62mm machine-gun is fitted in the centre of the glacis plate and is controlled by the driver. In recent years, many tanks have had this gun removed and the firing point blanked over due to the dubious utility of such a weapon. The driver is provided with two periscopes for viewing when the tank is buttoned up, and the seat is easily adjustable to raise the driver's head outside the hatch when not in combat zones. A hood and windscreen are carried for use by the driver in bad weather.

The turret arrangement of the T-54 is unconventional in several respects. As on the T-34-85 and T-44, the gunner and commander occupy the left half of the turret, and the loader occupies the right, the reverse to Western practice. The turret is not fitted with a basket, but the crew is suspended above the hull floor on seats. The turret is so cramped that the gunner nearly sits in the commander's lap. The bulky D-10T gun takes up a large portion of the turret's internal space and further congestion is caused by a ready-rack for ammunition stowage along the rear wall.

The fire controls for the armament are considerably simpler than those used on comparable foreign types. While the United States and West Germany have favoured an optical coincidence or stereoscopic rangefinder (and currently a laser rangefinder) and Britain a ranging rifle set-up, the Soviet Army has stuck to a simple stadiametric system. To engage a target, the tank commander locates a target using his TPK-1 designator sight and swings the turret roughly in line. Using the ranging graticule on his sight, the commander estimates range, informs the gunner of the type of ammunition to be used and the range of the target. The gunner takes over, fine aims the D-10T with his TSh-22 articulated telescope and fires. Should another shot be needed, the gun must be fully elevated to give the loader room to extract the spent casing and reload, and the gun must be resighted. The main drawback to this layout, apart from the time-consuming reloading procedure, is the relative inaccuracy of a stadiametric system compared to other methods, particularly at longer ranges. At close ranges, the system does allow for quick reaction time.

As production continued, the D-10T was refined. In 1955, a new version of the basic T-54 appeared which, in

the West, is usually designated T-54A. It was fitted with the newer D-10TG gun, which was gyro-stabilized along the vertical axis and had power elevation. It can be easily distinguished from preceding models by the small counterweight fitted at the fore end of the main gun to compensate for the stabilizer. Later, a bore evacuator was fitted. Internally, the vehicle had new air filters, an electric oil pump, a bilge pump for wading and snorkelling, an automatic fire extinguisher layout, and it was eventually fitted with additional external fuel cells. About two years later, additional refinements led to the very similar T-54B. Once again, the major changes were internal. A new model of the 100mm main armament was fitted, the D-10T2S, which had stabilization in both planes, derived from similar units on US Lend-Lease equipment. For the first time, infra-red night vision equipment was provided for the tank commander and gunner as a standard production feature. Other features included improved snorkel gear. The final major production type was given the US Army designation T-54X to signify its transitional role between the T-54 and T-55 family. The T-54X was essentially the same as the T-54B, but dispensed with the turret 12.7mm Degtaryev anti-aircraft machine-gun and cupola and featured a simple flush loader's hatch instead.

The T-54X was followed shortly afterwards by the T-55, which was first shown publicly at a parade in Moscow on 7 November 1961. This tank did not differ from the preceding T-54 series in any major respect, but basically represented a culmination in the technical improvements begun in the early 1950s. The major refinements in the T-55 were the uprated V-55 engine, an improved transmission and a rotating turret floor. The only external difference between a T-54X and a T-55 is the T-55's lack of the large circular roof vent forward of the loader's hatch. This vent is the key feature in distinguishing T-54s from T-55s.

With the introduction of the T-55, many of the earlier T-54s were re-manufactured or refitted with the new modifications, particularly the L-2G infra-red searchlight and complementary vision devices. Some were also fitted with two-plane stabilization. Most notable among these retrofits were the T-54(M) and T-54A(M).

At the 1963 May Day Parade, the final major mutation of the T-55 family, the T-55A, was first seen. The T-55A differed from the preceding model in having raised covers and anti-radiation lining over the two turret hatches and over the driver's position. The T-55A dispensed with the hull machine-gun, though many later production T-55s also had this modification and many other earlier types had it removed during repair. The space taken up by the machine-gun and its ammunition allowed the T-55A to carry six more rounds of 100mm ammunition. Although the standard production models of both the T-55 and T-55A were not fitted with the Degtaryev 12.7mm anti-aircraft machine-gun, many have subsequently been retrofitted with this feature, and are designated T-55(M) and T-55A(M), respectively. This was done largely in reaction

Right: The third, and standard, production series of the T-54 resembles this vehicle of the Finnish Army. It has the distinctive horse-shoe crab-shaped turret, the 'pig snout' mantlet and the early D-10T without infra-red gear. The Dushka anti-aircraft machine-gun is evident, as is the turret dome ventilator below it; this latter feature is the primary external distinction between the T-54 and T-55. (Kalevi Moilanen)

Top: A Czechoslovak T-54A enters a shallow stream with snorkel gear during the Warsaw Pact's 'Vltava' exercises in southern Bohemia. Due to the shallowness of the river, only half the snorkel has been fitted, but the covers over the exhaust ports are closed. The Czechoslovak Army is the only force in the Warsaw Pact to make systematic use of disruptive paint camouflage on its armoured vehicles. It has several official schemes for the various seasons of the year.

Centre: The T-55A was the first version of the T-54/55 family to be fitted with a radiation/biological filter system. This is externally evident by the prominent plastic-lined radiation covers fitted over the driver's, commander's and loader's hatches; as can be seen on these T-55As from a tank battalion in the southern Ukraine in 1975. The searchlight, which appears to be facing rearwards on the back of the turret, is in fact a night position light, which flashes the vehicle number (383) to the driver behind. (Sovfoto)

Below: This excellent view of an early production T-55, taken in the Volga Military District in 1974, shows all the distinctive details of this new series. The loader's flush hatch, like that on the T-54X, cannot be fitted with a Dushka anti-aircraft machine-gun. The absence of a turret ventilator dome in front of this hatch clearly identifies it as a T-55. The small port for the fixed hull machine-gun, in the middle of the glacis plate below the splash panel, was a feature found only on T-54s and early production T-55s. This vehicle is fitted with a full array of infra-red searchlights and sighting devices. (Sovfoto)

Right: In view of the threat posed by NATO tactical strike aircraft, many T-55s and T-55As were refitted with turret Dushka anti-aircraft machine-guns. This particular group of vehicles consists of three T-55(M), followed by a single unmodified T-55. The T-55(M) can be distinguished from the similar T-55A(M) by the absence of turret hatch radiation covers over the commander's and driver's positions. (Sovfoto)

Right: T-55A(M)s participating in the Yug (South) exercises in June 19/1. While these vehicles are similar in appearance to the T-55(M) they can be distinguished by the thickened plastic-lined hatches and hatch covers. Most of the refitted T-55s have additional ammunition containers for the Dushka AA machine-gun stored externally in canvas-protected magazines. (Sovfoto)

Left: This T-55 of the Czechoslovak Army is fitted with both a narrow combat snorkel forward of the loader's hatch, and a wide training snorkel over the loader's hatch. The training snorkel is used to acquaint crews with river-crossing techniques, and provides them with a means of escape should a mechanical failure or obstacle strand them in mid-stream.

Right top: The command version of the T-55 can only be identified if the rear is visible, as in this view. A small tubular rack containing additional radio aerials for the command sets is fitted at the rear of the hull above the unditching beam. (Kalevi Moilanen via Karl Rosenlof)

Right centre: A Polish Army T-54A towing a Star 660 heavy truck out of a river. The glossy black rubber seals over the gun telescope port and turret ventilator are quite evident, as is the narrow combat snorkel. (Joseph Desautels)

Right bottom: The Chinese T-59 is an exact copy of the T-54A and, from photographs alone, it is almost impossible to tell them apart. This T-59 was captured in South Vietnam. Surprisingly, it is fitted with an old German Notek driving light as well as the usual Soviet-style ones. During the Vietnam War, the T-54, T-59 and PT-76 were the most commonly encountered North Vietnamese tanks. (US Army)

T-55A(M) medium tank

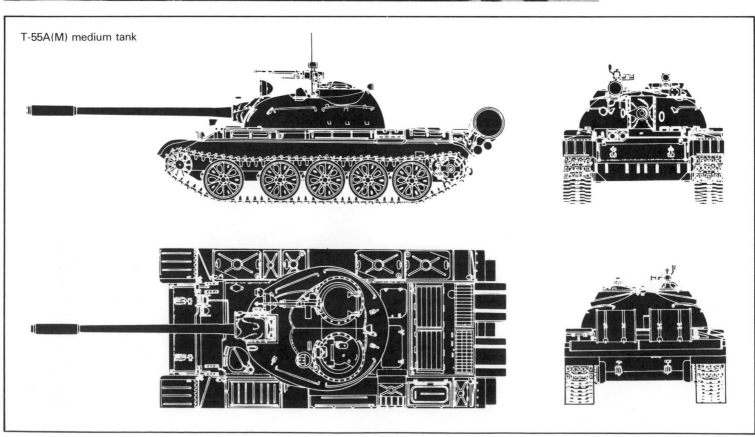

T-55A(M) MEDIUM TANK

Weight: 36 tonnes
Crew: 4 (driver, gunner, loader and commander)
Length, overall: 29.5ft (9m)
Length of hull: 21ft (6.45m)
Width: 11ft (3.27m)
Height: 8ft (2.4m)
Ground clearance: 17in (432mm)
Fuel capacity:
Internal: 128 gallons (580 litres)
Basic external: 84 gallons (380 litres)
Supplementary external: 88 gallons (400 litres)
Fuel Consumption:
Road: .63mpg (1.8 litres per km)
Cross-country: .98mpg (2.8 litres per km)
Range: 310 miles (500km)
Maximum speed: 30mph (50km/hr)
Maximum gradient: 30°
Trench crossing: 9ft (2.7m)
Vertical obstruction: 32in (80cm)
Unprepared fording: 56in (140cm)
Snorkelling: 14ft (5.5m)
Ground pressure: 11.52psi (.81kg/cm²)
Engine: V-55 diesel; 580hp at 2,000rpm; V-12; water-cooled
Armament:
Main gun: D-10T2S 100mm rifled gun with two-plane stabilization; −4° to 17° elevation
Ammunition stowed: 40 rounds
Ammunition: HE projectile/round weight 34lbs/— (15.7kg/—), initial muzzle velocity 2,995ft/sec (900m/s)
APHE projectile/round weight 35lbs/— (15.9kg/—), initial muzzle velocity 3,282ft/sec (1,000m/sec)
HVAP details not known
HEAT projectile/round weight 27lbs/— (12.2kg), initial muzzle velocity 2,955ft/sec (900m/s)
Armour penetration: APHE 7¼in (185mm)
HVAP not known
HEAT 15in (380mm)
Supplementary armament: Coaxial 7.62mm PKT machine-gun; 12.7mm DShK anti-aircraft machine-gun; 3,500 rounds of machine-gun ammunition stowed
Fire control and vehicle vision devices:
Commander: TPK-1 designator
Gunner: TSh2A-22 telescope and an infra-red TPN 1-41-11 periscope
General: An infra-red L-2G main searchlight with OU-3GK searchlight on the commander's hatch
Armour:
Glacis plate: 4in (100mm)
Upper hull side: 2¾in (70mm)
Mantlet: 6¾in (170mm)

to increased Western interest in tactical strike aircraft and assault helicopters.

There are some reports that a special export model of the T54/55 family has been produced with thinner hull armour, but this has not been confirmed. Both the T-54 and T-55 were produced in Czechoslovakia and Poland in a number of different versions. Many of the Polish-built machines, which also serve with other Warsaw Pact armies, such as that of East Germany, can be distinguished by the large stowage bin fitted to the left side of the turret.

The People's Republic of China produces an unlicensed copy of the T-54, designated T-59, which is essentially similar to the basic T-54 but with some simplifications. China also produces two AFVs in the light tank category that strongly resemble the T-54. The first of these, the T-62 light tank (not to be confused with the Soviet T-62 medium tank), is essentially a T-54 with thinner armour, fitted with an 85mm gun and narrower tracks. The T-63 is a peculiar 4/5 scale mimic of the T-54, using the turret from the T-60 light amphibious tank with an 85mm gun, and the running gear of the K-63 armoured troop carrier.

The T-54/55 family has been used as the basis for a number of self-propelled guns, tractors, bridging vehicles and armoured recovery vehicles. It has been built in larger quantities than any other post-war tank and has probably even exceeded the prodigious output of its predecessor, the T-34, which totalled at least 60,000 vehicles, not

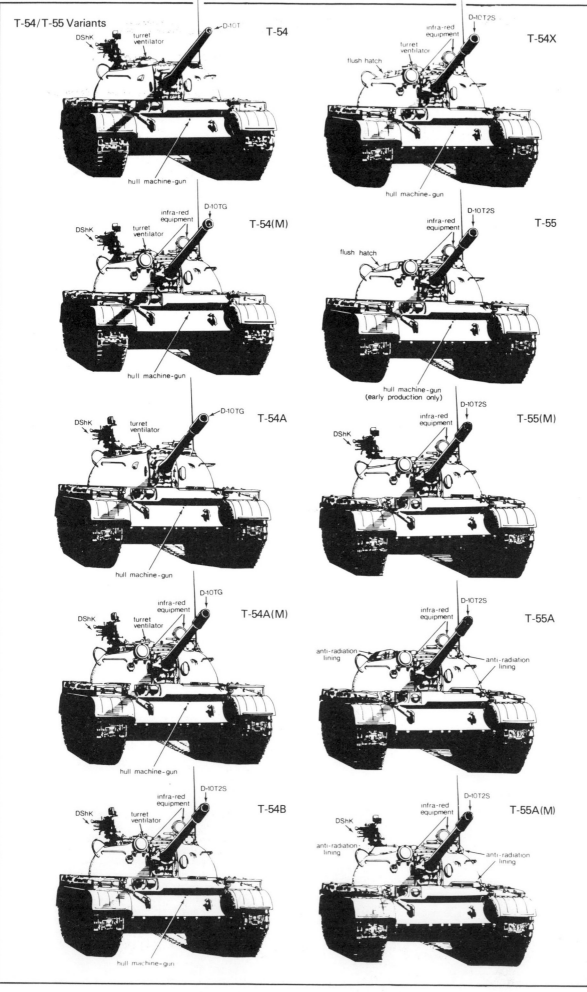

T-54/T-55 Variants

T-54 — DShK, turret ventilator, D-10T, hull machine-gun

T-54X — flush hatch, turret ventilator, infra-red equipment, D-10T2S, hull machine-gun

T-54(M) — DShK, turret ventilator, infra-red equipment, D-10TG, hull machine-gun

T-55 — flush hatch, infra-red equipment, D-10T2S, hull machine-gun (early production only)

T-54A — DShK, turret ventilator, D-10TG, hull machine-gun

T-55(M) — DShK, infra-red equipment, D-10T2S

T-54A(M) — DShK, turret ventilator, infra-red equipment, D-10TG, hull machine-gun

T-55A — infra-red equipment, D-10T2S, anti-radiation lining, anti-radiation lining

T-54B — DShK, turret ventilator, infra-red equipment, D-10T2S, hull machine-gun

T-55A(M) — DShK, infra-red equipment, D-10T2S, anti-radiation lining, anti-radiation lining

Right: Two views of a T-54 captured by the Israeli Army. (US Army)

16

Left, top: Front view of a T-54.

Left, bottom: A T-54 moving off.

Right: The last two Arab-Israeli conflicts have left the Israeli Army with about 400 T-54 and T-55s in working order. Both types are very unpopular due to their cramped internal arrangements and poor automotive life. Many have been re-manufactured and designated Ti-67. The most important modification was the substitution of the NATO 105mm gun for the inferior D-10 100mm gun. (The two T-54s shown here are both fitted with the 105mm NATO gun.) A significant number of T54/55s have been sold to the United States Army for training purposes. (US Army)

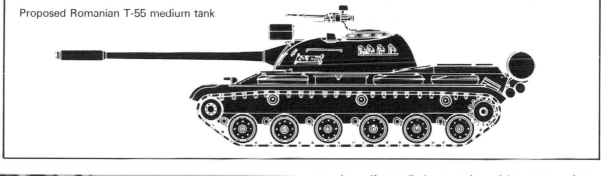

Proposed Romanian T-55 medium tank

Below: A major factor in retarding the T-54 and T-55s effective rate of fire is the awkward loading arrangement in the tank. The very large size of the rounds for the D-10 gun can be seen in this photograph, showing three Czechoslovak tankers loading F-412 high explosive rounds aboard a T-54. Usually, a tank carries a mixture of BR-412 armour piercing rounds and F-412 Frag-HE rounds.

counting self-propelled gun and special purpose variants. As such, it is the most widely produced tank in history. In comparison, the total output of the post-war American tank family of the M-26, M-46, M-47, M-48 and M-60 amounted to only about 28,000 vehicles. Some estimates of the T-54/55's sixteen-year production run places the final total at well over 100,000 vehicles.

Not surprisingly, the T-54/55 types have seen extensive combat around the globe. The T-54 saw some action in the bloody fighting in Budapest during the 1956 Hungarian uprising, and subsequently saw combat duty in the Indo-Pakistani Wars, the Sino-Soviet border clashes, the Vietnam War, the Vietnam-Cambodia War, the 1967 and 1973 Arab-Israeli conflicts, the 1970 Palestine Liberation Organization-Jordanian fighting, the Ethiopian and Angolan fighting, and in several coup d'états. The Chinese-built T-59s have served with the North Vietnamese Army against the American, South Vietnamese and Cambodian armies, with the Chinese against the Soviets and with the Pakistanis against the Indians. Both the T-54 and T-55 have been exported as far afield as Peru.

Some recipient countries have not been overly pleased with the design, citing poor manufacturing standards and difficulties in obtaining spares. Although cheaper than comparable Western tanks, both the T-54 and the T-55 have noticeably shorter active service lives and in some respects are designed more for replacement than major rebuilding. Romania has had such serious problems with its T-54s that it approached several West German firms for bids to completely rework the existing vehicles, adding new suspension, track, wheels, engine and other components. While this is by far the most blatant example of consumer unrest amongst the USSR's military clients, the Poles and Czechoslovaks make no secret of the fact that they consider their locally produced models to be distinctly superior to the Ural original.

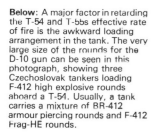

The T-62

In 1965, the T-62 medium tank made its first public appearance. The T-62 programme served the same basic purpose as the comparable US M-48/M-60 transition. Both programmes used existing components of successful tanks to create a new main battle tank equipped with a superior gun. In the case of the T-62, the leap was made from a conventional rifled gun, the D-10T, to the smoothbore U-5T. The U-5T fires a superb hypervelocity, fin-stabilized round that has excellent armour penetration capabilities, thereby justifying the design of a new vehicle to fit it. Nevertheless, the parentage of the T-55 is very obvious.

Many of the features added to the later T-55s were not part of the original conception. In contrast, the T-62 was designed from the outset with these features in mind. Among these are the PAZ nuclear defence system and the OPVT snorkel layout. The PAZ system was first factory-fitted on the T-55A. An RBZ-1m gamma ray detector

triggers the network, hermetically sealing the vehicle against airborne contaminants by use of air filters, hatch lining and an overpressure system. Biological and chemical contaminants can similarly be excluded.

In common with the T-55 and later T-54s, the T-62 is designed to accept the OPVT snorkel system for use in underwater river crossings. The Soviet Ground Forces have always taken a greater interest in unconventional river crossing techniques than have Western European armies, due to their bloody experiences in the 1944 and 1945 assaults. Russian experiments in the field date back to the T-26PKh and BT-5PKh of the late 1930s. To use the system, the tank is sealed with rubber gaskets, metal covers and caulking, and a snorkel tube is fitted to the turret and tied down with stays. This procedure can take from between fifteen minutes and eight hours, depending upon how thorough the job is done, which system is being used and how much faith the crew has in the bilge pump.

T-62A MEDIUM TANK
Weight: 40 tonnes
Crew: 4 (driver, gunner, loader and commander)
Length, overall: 31ft (9.335m)
Length of hull: 22ft (6.63m)
Width: 11ft (3.30m)
Height: 8ft (2.395m)
Ground clearance: 17in (432mm)
Fuel capacity:
Internal: 148 gallons (675 litres)
Basic external: 63 gallons (285 litres)
Supplementary external: 88 gallons (400 litres)
Fuel consumption:
Road: .85mpg (.30 litres per km)
Range: 186-279 miles (300-450km)
Maximum speed: 30mph (50km/hr)
Maximum gradient: 30°
Trench crossing: 9ft (2.85m)
Vertical obstruction: 32in (80cm)
Unprepared fording: 55in (140cm)
Snorkelling: 14ft (5.5m)
Ground pressure: 10.24psi (0.72kg/cm²)
Engine: V-55 diesel; 580hp at 2,000rpm; V-12; water-cooled
Armament:
Main gun: U-5T 115mm smoothbore gun with two-plane stabilization; −3° to +17° elevation
Ammunition stowed: 40 rounds
Ammunition: BR-6 APDS projectile/round weight 15lbs/50lbs (6.8kg/22.5kg), initial muzzle velocity 5,301ft/sec (1,615m/sec)
BK-6 HEAT projectile/round weight 26lbs/58lbs

(11.8kg/26.2kg), initial muzzle velocity 3,282ft/sec (1,000m/s)
OF-18 Frag-HE projectile/round weight 39lbs/62lbs (17.7kg/28.1kg), initial muzzle velocity 2,460ft/sec (750m/s)
OF-11 Frag-HE projectile/round weight 39lbs/62lbs (17.7kg/28.1kg), initial muzzle velocity 2,562ft/sec (780m/s)
Armour penetration: BR-6 APDS fired at 1,000m (1,094yds) at 0°/60° 9in(228mm)/7⅞in (199mm); fired at 2,188yds (2,000m) at 0°/60° 5¾in (147mm)/5in (129mm)
BK-6 HEAT fired at 1,000m (1,094yds) at 0°/60° 19½in (495mm)/9¾in (248mm); fired at 2,000m (2,188yds) at 0°/60° 19½in (495mm)/9¾in (248mm)
Supplementary armament: Coaxial PKT 7.62mm machine-gun; 12.7mm DShK anti-aircraft machine-gun; 2,200 rounds of 7.62mm and 500 rounds of 12.7mm ammunition stowed
Fire control and vehicle vision devices:
Commander: TKN-3 designator sight
Gunner: TSh2B-41U telescope; an infra-red TPN 1-41-22M periscope. Some vehicles are fitted with an infra-red IPN-22M passive starlight scope with an effective range of 766-985yds (700-900m)
General: An infra-red L-2G main searchlight with OU-3GK searchlight on commander's cupola
Armour:
Glacis plate: 4in (100mm)
Upper hull side: 2¾in (70mm)
Mantlet: 6¾in (170mm)

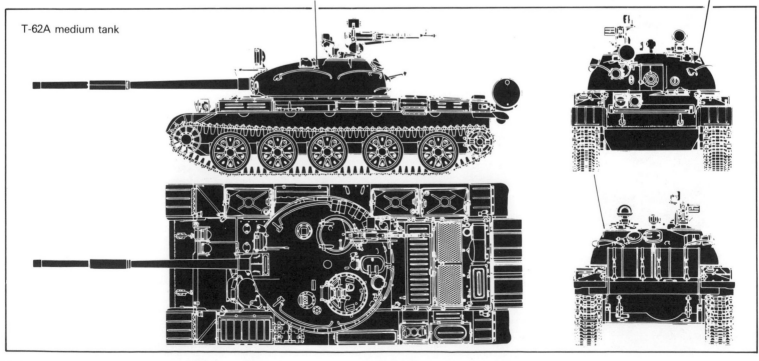

T-62A medium tank

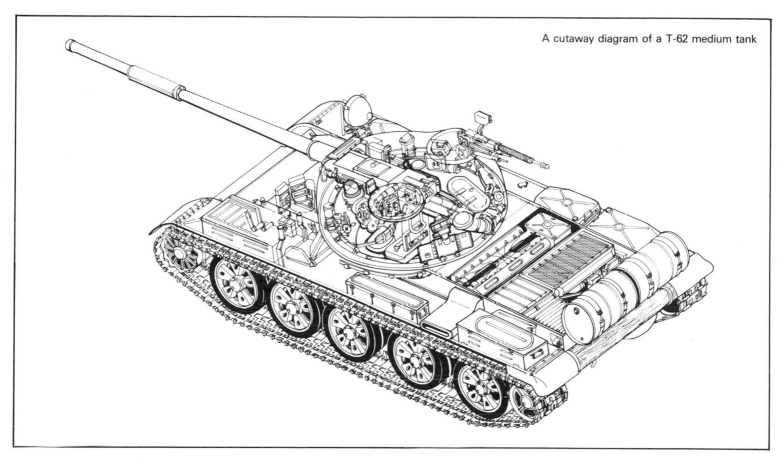

A cutaway diagram of a T-62 medium tank

The tank can only enter a river if the river bank is very low and can only exit under similar conditions. Optimally, the river bed should be reasonably firm and without excessive natural obstructions. The snorkel allows the tank to cross rivers up to 18ft deep (5.5m) and about 1,000yds wide (1km). Steering underwater is done with the aid of a GPK-59 gyro-compass, supplemented by radio instructions from the shore. The tank bilge pump can drain 22 gallons (100 litres) of water per minute. Once out of the river, the tank can be prepared for combat in a minute and a half.

There are obvious natural and psychological obstacles to the use of this device. Poor surface conditions on the river bed can easily strand a tank in mid-stream with fatal consequences for the crew. A small unseen gully or other obstruction can have the same dire results, although the use of a BTS-2 armoured recovery vehicle with a power winch might help in some cases. Not surprisingly, Soviet tank crews were not overly enthusiastic about the device, and after a few inevitable training accidents, they developed a special training tube, which allows the crew to evacuate in the event of problems. Usual training practice in some Warsaw Pact countries is to first familiarize the crew with the basic techniques by using a shallow man-made concrete water tank.

Initially, the T-54 used BDSh smoke canisters, but subsequently a thermal smoke system was devised and is fitted on the T-62. This ingenious system sprays diesel fuel into the exhaust manifold resulting in a 275-450yd (250-400m) long opaque smokescreen with an opacity of about 2-4 minutes. The system can operate for about 10 minutes and consumes about 2 gallons (10 litres) of fuel per minute.

Later production T-62s, designated T-62A, have a number of refinements, most noticeably a revised loader's hatch area, which is now fitted with a 12.7mm DShK machine-gun. Recently, two other models appeared: the T-62K and the T-62M. The T-62K is a command version, with extra radios, and can be fitted with a very tall radio mast when stationary. It carries more radio equipment than the standard tank, but less ammunition, an auxiliary generator and TNA-3 land navigation device. The T-62M is essentially similar to the T-62A but is fitted with the track and drive sprocket of the newer T-72. Many small changes are currently being introduced on T-62s, with priority going to those in the Group of Soviet Forces, Germany. These include the replacement of the L-2G infra-red searchlight

Above: The family resemblance between the sleek T-62 and the earlier T-55 is quite evident. The T-62 in the middle of this photograph (No. 193) has a snorkel tube lashed on top of the 44-gallon spare (200-litre) fuel drums at the hull rear. This tank and the T-62 in the background (No. 123) have their thermal smoke emitters activated. The diamond-shaped tactical marking visible on the turret sides of Nos. 185 and 193 is fairly common in tank units, being derived from the traditional tank symbol used on maps. (Sovfoto)

Left: The newest version of the T-62, the T-62M, is basically similar to the T-62A, but has the new drive sprocket and tracks of the T-72. The large, extra fuel drums are very evident in this view. The rectangular port outlined in white at fender level is the exhaust port for the engine. The three rounds of ammunition displayed at the front of the left fender are, from left to right, the BR-6 high velocity fin stabilized armour piercing round, the OF-18 fragmentation-high explosive round and the BK-6 high explosive anti-tank round. (US Army)

with a new model, the fitting of a laser rangefinder and ballistic computer and the addition of night-light intensification sights (starlight scopes).

It is quite curious that the T-62 has not been adopted by the other armies of the Warsaw Pact. This may have been due to its high unit cost as compared to the T-55, or it may have been prompted by the decision to develop so quickly a replacement for the T-62 in the form of the T-64/72 series. Rather than adopt the T-62, those Warsaw Pact armies with a priority status, respectively Poland, East Germany and Czechoslovakia, may have opted to wait for the T-64 or T-72.

The T-62 has been exported in very large numbers to the Egyptian and Syrian armies, and saw combat in 1967 and 1973. There are reports that the Bulgarians are receiving T-62s which, in view of the low priority given the Bulgarian Army, is all the more evidence that the Poles, East Germans and Czechs will receive newer types.

The T-64 and T-72

Soviet tank designers have recognized the limits of their mechanical creations and have had a chance to examine first-hand many of the contemporary NATO types, such as the M-48, M-60 and Centurion, captured by their allies in South-East Asia and the Middle East. The results of these efforts have become apparent in the past few years. By 1975, about 800 of the new T-64 main battle tank had been issued to the Category I divisions of the Group of Soviet Forces, Germany, with about another 1,200 stationed in European Russia. Estimates in 1978 put the figure at about 2,000 in the Group of Soviet Forces, Germany alone. At the November 1977 parade celebrating the 60th anniversary of the Bolshevik Revolution, an even more recent development was revealed for the first time, the T-72 main battle tank.

While a single new main battle tank had been expected by NATO analysts, the introduction of two related but significantly different types in so short a time came as a real surprise. It is possible, if not altogether likely, that the T-64 has been in service in European Russia for much longer

than since 1975. Even so, it is unclear why it would have been introduced into service in large numbers with the Group of Soviet Forces, Germany if it had shortcomings serious enough to warrant the development of a replacement design in the form of the T-72. Other speculation maintains that the two types are parallel designs and that one or another will be standardized. It is equally possible that this decision has already been reached and the runner-up is being widely displayed to confuse Western Intelligence. Some NATO analysts became very suspicious after the Soviets allowed the visiting French Minister of Defence to inspect closely a new T-72 at a Moscow area base in October 1977. Secrecy in the Soviet Army has been so great in the past that it was only recently that the Soviets officially acknowledged that the designation of the T-62 was in fact T-62.

Much of the data on the T-64 and T-72 are still speculative, but some observations can be made. The two major areas of improvement in these types over the previous T-62 are in the armament and mobility sectors. The major tactical flaw of the T-62 was that it could not

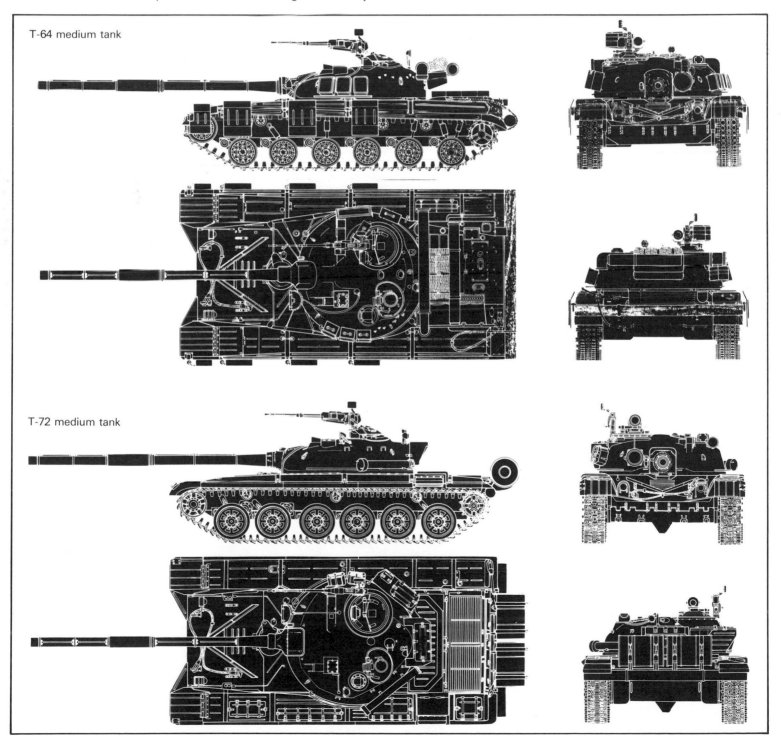

T-64 medium tank

T-72 medium tank

23

keep pace with the new BMP infantry combat vehicle (Bronevaya Maschina Piekhota). Its speed was limited by its modified Christie suspension. At high speeds, in fact, it tends to set up harmonic vibrations, which give a poor ride and can literally shake apart certain components. The suspension system used on the T-62 had been developed to the limit of its potential. Furthermore, the V-55 engine, which is basically only an uprated version of the V-2 diesel in use since the BT-7M and T-34 of the 1939-40 period, had also been pushed very near to its limit. There are some unconfirmed reports that the Soviets attempted to get around the problem by testing modified examples of the T-62 with a conventional live track and return-roller arrangement (probably designated as T-67 and T-68), but the designers could not escape the fact that a larger hull was needed to accommodate an improved power plant.

Concurrently, a layered composite armour, known as Chobham armour, was being developed in Britain. Unlike conventional steel armour, Chobham armour seems to consist of several layers of nylon micromesh or ceramic bonded on either side with a titanium alloy armour plate. Tests on the armour have revealed that it is able to laterally disperse the fiery tongue of a shaped charge blast within the nylon micromesh, thereby rendering most of the current generation of wire guided anti-tank missiles and infantry anti-tank rockets useless. This is all the more important in view of the considerable success scored by Egyptian anti-tank gunners in 1973 using the 9M14M 'Sagger' anti-tank missile against Israeli tanks. The armour also seems to be quite effective against many conventional kinetic energy rounds such as the standard APDS types.

T-64 MEDIUM TANK (provisional data)
Weight: 38 tonnes
Crew: 3 (driver, gunner and commander)
Length, overall: 30ft (9.02m)
Length of hull: 21ft (6.35m)
Width: 11ft (3.375m)
Height: 7ft (2.265m)
Ground clearance: 14½in (370mm)
Range: 310 miles (500km)
Maximum speed: 62mph (100km/hr)
Engine: 750hp diesel
Armament:
Main gun: 125mm smoothbore
Rate of fire: 4 rounds per minute
Ammunition stowed: APFSDS 12 rounds; HEAT 6 rounds; HE 22 rounds
Ammunition: APFSDS 5,301ft/sec (1,615m/sec)
HEAT details not known
HE details not known
Supplementary armament: Coaxial 7.62mm machine-gun; 12.7mm anti-aircraft machine-gun
Armour:
Glacis plate: 4in (100mm)
Upper hull side: 2¾in (70mm)

T-72 MEDIUM TANK (provisional data)
Weight: 41 tonnes
Crew: 3 (gunner, driver, commander)
Length, overall: 30ft (9.24m)
Length of hull: 23ft (6.95m)
Width: 11ft (3.375m)
Height: 8ft (2.37m)
Ground clearance: 17in (420mm)
Range: 310 miles (500km)
Maximum speed: 62mph (100km/hr)
Engine: 750hp diesel
Armament:
Main gun: 125mm smoothbore
Rate of fire: 4 rounds per minute
Ammunition stowed: APFSDS 12 rounds; HEAT 6 rounds; HE 22 rounds
Ammunition: APFSDS 5,301ft/sec (1,615m/sec)
HEAT details not known
HE details not known
Supplementary armament: Coaxial 7.62mm machine-gun; 12.7mm anti-aircraft machine-gun
Armour:
Glacis plate: 4in (100mm)
Upper hull side: 2¾in (70mm)

Left: This overhead view of the new T-64 medium tank shows the circular shape of the turret, as well as the very long thermally insulated barrel of the 125mm gun. The T-64 is armed with a new model 14.5mm anti-aircraft machine-gun, which is seen here shrouded in canvas. At the turret rear is a large stowage bin and one of the two snorkels. (US Army)

Left: The T-64 has considerably more external stowage than have previous Soviet medium tanks. Much of this consists of the sleek fender panniers, which are used mainly for fuel stowage. The containers around the turret contain ammunition for the machine-gun, and the crew's personal gear and tools. (US Army)

Left: The T-64K is the command version of the basic T-64. During operations, it must remain stationary if the high radio mast fitted to the turret roof is to be properly fastened down with stays. Unlike the basic tank version, the T-64K is not fitted with a heavy machine-gun over the commander's hatch at the right. It has additional racks to stow fuel drums on the engine deck. This particular vehicle has both sets of snorkels fitted on their stowage mounts behind the turret. (US Army)

Below, left: Unlike previous medium tanks, the T-64 uses two sets of snorkels for crossing river beds underwater. One feeds the engine, while the other, which is attached over the gunner's hatch, is for the crew. Due to the automatic loader, the turret crew positions in the T-64 have shifted, with the commander on the right and the gunner farther back in the left turret cavity. (US Army)

Above, right: This T-72 has gill armour fitted to the fenders and splayed out in battle position. Below the nose plate, the integral bulldozer blade can be seen in the 'down' position. The tube on the turret rear is the turret snorkel. The T-72 seems to use only a single combat snorkel instead of the two used by the T-64. (US Army)

Right: A T-72 on its way to the parade in Moscow in November 1977. The barrel is locked in its travelling position. Also evident is the insulated sleeve over the barrel. The T-72 has far more sophisticated fire controls than the older T-62. (US Army)

Improved Chobham-style armour is being used on several of the new NATO tank types, such as the Bundeswehr's Leopard II and the American M-1. Ironically, Chobham armour is so expensive that the British themselves are not yet adopting it.

In response to this revolutionary development, the Soviets accelerated their work on an enlarged version of the T-62's excellent U-5T gun, increasing it from 115mm to 125mm. The T-62's turret ring could not accept a larger piece, so a wholly new tank design was needed.

While creating the new vehicle, Soviet designers took the opportunity to eliminate the serious loading system flaw in their earlier tanks by providing an automatic loading system similar to that used on the BMP. Unlike the loaders on the AMX-13, Leopard II or M-1, which place their rounds in a bustle at the turret rear, the Soviet system puts the rounds in a circular clip at the base of the turret basket. This allows for a far more compact turret, but it does lead to a slower rate of fire.

The fire controls on the T-64/72 family seem to be identical and probably consist of a coincidence rangefinder, ruby laser rangefinder, a conventional stadiametric rangefinder as a backup and an analogue ballistic computer. Some of these features will no doubt be fitted to the T-62M and the T-62A(M) later. Coupled with a light intensification sight, these advances would go a long way towards narrowing the gunnery gap between Warsaw Pact and NATO armour. It remains to be seen, however, if the Soviets are willing to invest enough money in each tank to add a sophisticated stabilizing system for the main gun, and thus provide a fire-on-the-move capability.

The T-64/72 family, like most Soviet tanks, have low, sleek, ballistically well shaped hulls. They are just as badly cramped inside as the T-62, but with the automatic loader and the likely fitting of boosted driver controls, these effects are mitigated. The exterior shape does not have the slab sided appearance of the Leopard II or M-1, which gives away the use of Chobham armour. It is likely that the Soviet Ground Forces will eventually introduce a T-72

variant with composite armour of some sort. Some sources have tentatively identified this new tank as the T-80. The T-64 and the T-72 can both be fitted with 'gill armour' or 'bat wings' along their flanks. This supplementary armour is a cheap expedient until a vehicle with full composite armour can be introduced. Gill armour helps degrade the performance of hostile anti-tank weapons firing shaped charge warheads at the front of the tank. The panels are spring loaded and splay out at about 65° to the hull, like fish gills. When viewed from a frontal quarter, slightly off-centre, they cover much of the running gear and parts of the turret and fender panniers.

It has been necessary to spring out these screens rather than fix them on in a stationary fashion, such as those on German and Hungarian tanks during the Second World War. This change was implemented to combat the improvement in bazooka-type weapons in the post-war years. In contrast to the wartime panzerfaust or bazooka, a modern weapon such as the RPG-7 would have its performance enhanced rather than degraded by the positioning of a stationary shield a few feet from the main armour. But in order to defeat the shaped charge used by modern infantry anti-tank weapons, the screens must be a considerable distance away from the main armour. When sprung outwards, the gill armour of the T-64 and T-72 detonates the rounds far enough away to dissipate the shaped charges' tongue of fire.

The main difference between the T-64 and T-72 is the running gear. While both use a conventional small road wheel/return-roller layout with live track, they do differ in other respects. The rear engine deck areas vary between both types, leading to some suspicion that they are powered by different engine types. The T-72's deck is far closer in appearance to that on the T-62 than on the T-64; perhaps an indication that this tank uses some uprated version of the V-55 engine. Both have nearly identical hull glacis plates, but the turret ring fitting and fender panniers differ. The turrets on both types are very similar but not identical, particularly in regards to stowage bins and small

detail fittings. The rear of the T-72 turret has a distinct bulge, while that on the T-64 is rounder. Both vehicles have the same dual-snorkel arrangement in place of the older OPVT system of the T-62. A command tank version of the T-64, the T-64K, has been identified, and there is probably a similar T-72 version.

The T-64 and T-72 have solved a lot of the problems inherent in the T-55 and T-62 tanks, and have narrowed the gap with NATO types. Their small size still means they will carry fewer rounds and will not be as adaptable to future improvements as the larger NATO tanks, but they will certainly be available in larger numbers. The US Army is planning to purchase 7,058 M-1 Abrams, which will enter production in the 1980s. By 1977 the Ural factories had produced at least 2,000 T-64s and, at an annual production rate of about 2,000 vehicles, by the end of the 1970s will easily match M-1 and Leopard production before either project has really got off the ground.

The PT-76

Although the ubiquitous PT-76 reconnaissance vehicle is not strictly speaking a battle tank, it is probably best to include it in this chapter. In 1943, the Red Army halted production of light tanks and, until the end of the war, used up available stocks of T-70s and Lend-Lease Valentines in the scouting role. Nevertheless, in the post-war years, Soviet Ground Forces conceded the utility of a fully tracked scout vehicle and in 1952 introduced the PT-76.

The PT-76 resembles a tank in all conventional aspects: that is, it has a fully enclosed turret-mounted gun and is fully tracked. However, its role is not that of a battle tank, but is strictly for scouting. It is used solely in reconnaissance companies and battalions and not in the Ground Forces tank battalions, though it is used in the Soviet and Polish naval infantries' amphibious tank platoons.

A unique feature of the PT-76 is that it is one of the very few fully amphibious tanks now in service in the world. It is propelled through the water by drawing in water through ports at the rear of the hull sides, and ejecting it at the rear. Its large boxy hull provides a reasonable degree of buoyancy for use in rivers and lakes, but, unlike the US LVT P-7 series of troop carriers, it is not really intended for use in heavy surf.

Left: An overhead view of a T-72 showing the pronounced bulge at the turret rear, which is the primary difference between the turrets of the T-64 and T-72. The various fittings on the glacis plate on the front of the vehicle allow for the addition of mine ploughs. (US Army)

Below, left: In February 1978 the Soviet Ground Forces conducted manoeuvres (code-named 'Berezina') in Belorussiya and invited a delegation from NATO. Here, a company of the new T-72 tanks execute an attack over snow. The tactical unit insignia of the vehicle in the foreground consists of a circle, with its bottom half solid white and a small '2' in the upper part. (Sovfoto)

Right: This side view of a T-72 shows several of the features that distinguish the T-72 from the T-64. The road wheels are larger and of a somewhat different pattern, the fuel panniers are shaped differently, and turret stowage is not the same. (US Army)

PT-76 AMPHIBIOUS TANK

Weight: 14 tonnes
Crew: 3 (driver, gunner and commander)
Length, overall: 25ft (7.6m)
Length of hull: 23ft (7m)
Width: 10ft (3m)
Height: 8ft (2.5m)
Ground clearance: 14½in (368mm)
Fuel capacity:
Internal: 55 gallons (250 litres)
Fuel Consumption:
Road: 2.85mpg (1 litre per km)
Range: 155 miles (250km) on land, 37-43 miles (60-70km) on water
Maximum speed: 27mph (44km/hr) on land, 6mph (10.2km/hr) on water
Maximum gradient: 38°
Trench crossing: 9ft (2.8m)
Vertical obstruction: 3.5ft (1.1m)
Ground pressure: 6.8psi (.5kg/cm²)
Engine: V-6 diesel; 240hp at 1,800rpm; water-cooled

Armament:
Main gun: D-56T or D-56TM 76.2mm L/42 rifled gun; —4.5° to 31° elevation
Ammunition stowed: 40 rounds
Ammunition: HE projectile weight 14lbs (6.2kg), initial muzzle velocity 2,232ft/sec (680m/sec)
HVAP projectile weight 7lbs (3.1kg), initial muzzle velocity 3,168ft/sec (965m/sec)
APHE projectile weight 14lbs (6.2kg), initial muzzle velocity 2,151ft/sec (655m/sec)
HEAT projectile weight 9lbs (4kg), initial muzzle velocity 1,050ft/sec (325m/sec)
Armour penetration: APHE fired at 1,000m (1,094yds) at 0° 2³⁄₈in (61mm)
HVAP fired at 1,000m (1,094yds) at 0° 2¼in (58mm)
HEAT fired at 1,000m (1,094yds) at 0° 4¾in (120mm)
Supplementary armament: Coaxial 7.62 SGMT; 1,000 rounds stowed
Armour:
Glacis plate: ³⁄₈in (11mm)
Upper hull side: ½in (14mm)
Mantlet: ³⁄₈in (11mm)

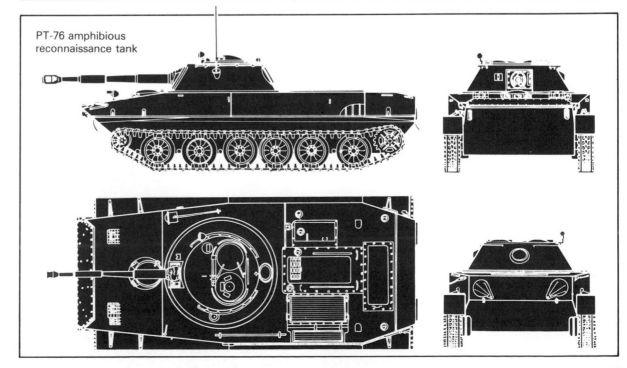

PT-76 amphibious reconnaissance tank

The main turret armament is either the D-56T with a multi-baffle muzzle brake on early production models, or the D-56TM with double-baffle brake on later types. Some Polish and Hungarian PT-76 have had the double-baffle muzzle brake removed. Not surprisingly, the PT-76 is very lightly armoured, at no point exceeding ½in (14mm), and its side armour can be penetrated by shell fragments and even .50 calibre AP machine-gun rounds. (PT-76s used in Vietnam were very vulnerable to air strikes.) Nevertheless, it gives the scout units of Soviet armoured and motorized rifle divisions a great deal of tactical mobility due to its excellent water crossing capabilities. There is evidence that the PT-76 is being replaced by a reconnaissance version of the BMP infantry combat vehicle.

The People's Republic of China produces a modified version of the PT-76 known as the T-60, which is fitted with a new turret, resembling a small scale T-54 turret, armed with an 85mm gun. The hull has also been redesigned to accommodate the greater weight of the new gun, but is similar in appearance. The basic chassis or components of the PT-76 have been used in a wide variety of other tracked vehicles, particularly armoured troop carriers and tactical nuclear missile launchers.

Comparison between Warsaw Pact and NATO battle tanks
It would take an inordinate amount of space to compare each type of Warsaw Pact tank against the wide variety of tank types fielded by the NATO forces. Nevertheless, it is possible to make some general observations. There is a great deal of difference between an early T-54 and the latest T-62M, just as there is a great deal of difference between an M-48 and an M-60A-2, so the limits of such remarks should be kept in mind.

The foremost advantage of Warsaw Pact tanks is their greater number. How great the difference is difficult to pin-point for many complicated reasons, but it is considerable no matter how the tally is made. The difficulties in calculation arise from whether Soviet non-European reserves are included, whether the French, Spanish, Romanian, or other armies are counted, and so on. Thus, estimates range from as high as 4:1 to about 2.5:1, with most analysts focussing on a 3:1 advantage. Figures like this are misleading, since they count and compare very unequal items. A worn-out T-54 is hardly equivalent to a well maintained Chieftain, and a new T-62 is not the same as an old rusted M-47 on its last legs. Perhaps an historical example will suffice to illuminate the pitfalls of relying on unqualified raw totals.

In 1941, when the Germans invaded the Soviet Union, the Red Army possessed about 23,000 tanks compared to less than 4,000 in the Wehrmacht's Panzer divisions. Contrary to popular historical misconception, the Soviet tanks were not significantly inferior to German types. In fact, most Red Army tank units were equipped with T-26s, BT-5s and BT-7s, which compared very favourably with the Germans machine-gun armed Pz Kpfw Is and Pz Kpfw IIs. Even if the obsolete Soviet types such as the T-27 are ignored, the Red Army enjoyed nearly a 5:1 advantage in tanks. Yet the 1941 débâcle occurred in spite of the rather startling numbers. What the figures did not reveal was that of the 23,000 Soviet tanks, 29 per cent required major rebuilding and 44 per cent needed major overhaul. Spare parts were difficult to obtain, and nearly three-quarters of the Soviet tank park was virtually incapacitated by a lack of repair facilities. The Soviets still enjoyed a numerical advantage, but this was quickly whittled away by the Germans superior tactics, training and morale.

It would be dangerous for Western defence planners to draw an immediate parallel between the situation in 1941 and the situation today. Yesterday's paper tiger bears little relation to the sinewy veteran of a brutal war we see today. But it is also facile to accept the raw figures of Warsaw Pact/NATO tanks as anything more than a shadow of the force it really represents. The Warsaw Pact advantage is quite real, but certainly not as startling as it might seem at first glance.

The smaller size of Soviet battle tanks gives them a notable tactical advantage over the larger and taller NATO types. They are fully three feet lower than the M-60 and, therefore, present smaller frontal targets to opposing gunners. Their armour is thick and well sloped. Recent firing tests in West Germany using the standard NATO

105mm gun against a T-62 found that only the high explosive anti-tank round (HEAT) was capable of regularly penetrating the frontal armour at a range of 1,000yds (1km). Several US rounds, notably the depleted uranium hyper-shot, are also capable of easily penetrating the T-62's frontal armour, but as of the time of writing, these were not available to US troops in Europe due to political factors. The depleted uranium rounds use dense, spent uranium cores instead of tungsten, but after the neutron bomb imbroglio, US politicians have proved wary of encouraging the adoption of any tactical weapon that smacks of being nuclear related, even if mistakenly so. The large 120mm gun of the Chieftain is capable of penetrating the T-62 with a variety of rounds, and even if the high explosive rounds are incapable of penetrating, they are large enough to wrench the tank apart or cause catastrophic spalling of the inner faces of the armour. The small size of Soviet medium tanks has less desirable side effects on the vehicles' performance, and this will be touched on subsequently.

The simple fire control system of Soviet tanks allows reasonably quick response at close ranges, which is an advantage, but at ranges beyond 1,000yds (1km), the simple stadiametric ranging method is inferior to those systems used on NATO types.

In comparison with NATO tanks, a far higher percentage of Soviet tanks are fitted with night-fighting equipment, and night combat is more heavily emphasized in the Warsaw Pact. Under optimum night conditions, a gunner in a T-55 or T-62 has an effective viewing range of 875yds (800m), the commander about 450yds (400m) and the driver roughly 45yds (40m). Recent tests in West Germany, however, indicate that starlight or intense moonlight can reduce the performance of these units.

One reason why NATO has been slow to fully adopt infra-red equipment is the realization that passive light intensification sights, which are just becoming technically and commercially feasible, are tactically superior to active infra-red systems. The IR searchlight on Soviet tanks can be detected easily by opposing anti-tank gunners using passive IR sights. In contrast, starlight scopes depend on ambient natural light from the moon and the stars and, since no searchlight is needed, they are not detectable. The Bundeswehr's Leopard is fitted with both a starlight scope and active IR, and the Soviet lead in night-fighting is being whittled away by the widespread introduction of these systems into other NATO countries. Some Soviet units in the Group of Soviet Forces, Germany are only now beginning to receive such light intensification scopes.

Soviet river crossing equipment is more widely available than comparable NATO equipment, and this gives the Warsaw Pact somewhat greater strategic and tactical mobility.

The armour-piercing, discarding-sabot rounds used in the D-10T and U-5T have an excellent chance of success against the armour of NATO tanks. The T-62's BR-6 APDS round can penetrate nearly 10 inches (254mm) of armour at a range of 1,000yds (1km), which is certainly quite sufficient against most current NATO types.

Unlike NATO, the Warsaw Pact countries have paid more attention to the potential use of tank guns in an indirect fire role, which offers somewhat more tactical flexibility. The D-10T has several effective high explosive/

shrapnel rounds available to it. To some extent, this development has been a necessary undertaking for the Soviets, in view of NATO's more widespread use of self-propelled artillery.

Soviet tanks, particularly those in Category I units, are more often fitted with NBC (Nuclear, Biological, Chemical) defence systems than are comparable NATO units. One curious feature of the Soviet system is that, when a radiologically contaminated area is reached, it automatically shuts off the tank's engine to warn the crew. The widespread use of the thermal smoke layer on Soviet tanks is in many respects superior to the smoke candle arrangement on NATO tanks.

Many of the aforementioned advantages that Soviet medium tanks possess over their NATO counterparts have been acquired by design compromises that in the long run degrade the overall performance of the vehicle. When built in larger numbers, workmanship is sometimes so poor as to require vehicle overhaul even before the tank has been issued to the troops. The Czech Army, before producing its own T-54s and T-55s, was quite startled to discover that, after only 25 hours of running, new Soviet-manufactured T-54s had deposited several ounces of metal filings in their crankcases. Engine overheating caused by poorly machined oil lines has been a problem and in some cases has limited effective engine life to only about 100 hours. Transmissions have never been a strong point in Soviet tanks, and the clutch accounts for 40 per cent of the mechanical breakdowns in the T-62 alone. Western defence analysts estimate that the T-62 has an average effective range of only about 100-125 miles (161-202km) before a serious mechanical failure, as compared to about 150-200 miles (241-322km) for most NATO tanks. On the older T-54s and T-55s, it can be assumed the situation is even worse. The fact that Soviet logistical support is still weak does not brighten the picture.

The small size of the T-55 and T-62 forced Soviet designers to mount a portion of the fuel externally. While diesel fuel does not have the explosive characteristics of petroleum, the externally mounted fuel panniers and drums are very vulnerable to fire from new automatic cannons, such as the 20mm on the Bundeswehr Marder troop carrier, or airborne weapons such as the 30mm Gatling on the American A-10. The light-weight V-55 diesel engine has a magnesium cast block, which, if ignited, makes a damaged vehicle totally irreparable.

Interior space on all the Soviet mediums is so cramped that it is impracticable to crew the vehicles with troops taller than 5 foot 5 inches. This situation would not be so bad if the vehicles were designed with a modicum of crew comfort or mechanical aids, but Soviet tanks are filled on the inside with small fittings and brackets that ensure that the crew will regularly be inflicted with bruises and gashes unless care is taken. While NATO tanks have their steering systems hydraulically boosted to cut down on driver fatigue, this is not the case in any of the Soviet-built T-55 or T-62 series. NATO troops who have driven the T-62 are highly critical of the great force required to steer the tank, and feel that this would seriously hamper a small driver under the usual trying combat conditions.

The most unenviable task is that of the gun loader. Even if the loader is rather short, his turret cavity is so small that

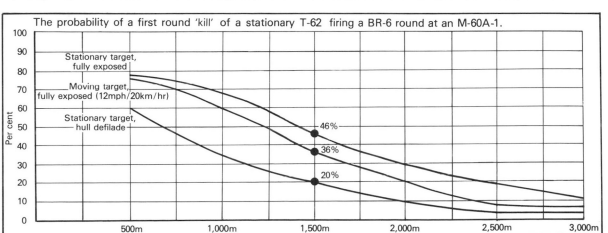

The probability of a first round 'kill' of a stationary T-62 firing a BR-6 round at an M-60A-1.

Stationary target, fully exposed

Moving target, fully exposed (12mph/20km/hr)

Stationary target, hull defilade

46%

36%

20%

Per cent — 100, 90, 80, 70, 60, 50, 40, 30, 20, 10, 0

500m   1,000m   1,500m   2,000m   2,500m   3,000m

he must remain seated or crouched. The rounds for the D-10T gun weigh well over 50 pounds (25kg), which would be difficult to manhandle even in the best of circumstances. But the T-55 loader not only has to manoeuvre these heavy, cumbersome rounds in a very cramped space, but he must ram them home with his left arm. Turret space is so limited that only three ready rounds can be carried in the turret, meaning that once these have been expended, the loader must perform acrobatics to obtain rounds from the racks at his feet or at knee level.

These tasks are especially dangerous when the gyro-stabilizer is turned on and the vehicle is in motion. While tracking a target, the gun breech and turret can unexpectedly swing about, pinioning or crushing the loader if he does not nimbly dodge it. Add to this the fact that spent shell casings litter the floor, making footing unsure, and the job becomes even less appealing. The T-62 has overcome at least the latter flaw, as shell casings are now automatically ejected through the rear of the turret.

The interior of the T-55 and T-62 is so small that the gun cannot be reloaded unless it is fully elevated. Once a round has been fired, the gun must be elevated, reloaded, and resighted. In the T-62, this is done automatically. Nevertheless, design compromises such as this, and the inefficient layout of the loader's position, seriously degrade the performance of the tank in action and result in a lower rate of fire than those of NATO tanks. These factors, combined with a springier suspension than on NATO types, inevitably lead to crew fatigue and motion and noise exhaustion.

Due to the cramped space, the T-62 carries only 40 rounds for the main gun as compared to 63 in the US M-60. It has also led to poor layout of vulnerable systems, particularly fuel and ammunition. A large fuel cell surrounds the ammunition bin under the right side of the glacis plate; Israeli tankers have found that even when their tank guns could not penetrate the armour of T-62s, a hit on that area often resulted in a 'catastrophic kill' when the fuel and ammunition detonated from the impact. Israeli gunners have also found that hits against the turret rear near the ready-racks often detonate the rounds, sometimes even with a non-penetrating glancing blow, with similarly dire results.

The turret traverse of the T-55 and T-62 is slower than on most NATO tanks, and this can have unfavourable results in close combat. The gun is placed so low in the turret that, due to the resultant restricted gun depression (only −4° on the T-55 and −3° on the T-62), a T-55 or T-62 cannot take full advantage of a hull-down or defilade position.

At ranges of 1,000yds (1km) or greater, the stadiametric ranging system is far less effective than the various NATO systems, and none of the T-55s or T-62s possess even a simple analogue ballistic computer. The Bundeswehr estimates that a T-62 has only about 16 per cent of the chance that the latest Leopard II has of hitting a stationary target at a range of 1,000yds (1km). In 'fine-grained' terrain, where tank combat takes place at short distances, Soviet tanks would not be at any disadvantage. In fact, at these ranges, the very flat trajectory of the T-62's BR-6 round obviates the need for sophisticated fire controls. But Soviet tanks would suffer in long-range engagements. The British Army feels that in such engagements, its Chieftain battle tank, which has the finest long-range capabilities of any current NATO tank, could expect a 4:1 'kill' ratio against T-62s. Not surprisingly, current Soviet doctrine maintains that a 4:1 superiority in tanks is needed to carry out any successful attack, and a minimum of 8:1 is needed along a main axis of attack.

Current Soviet tank gunnery has virtually no fire-on-the-move capability. The gun stabilization system in the T-55 and T-62 is so rudimentary that it is really useful only for pointing the gun in the right general direction to save time when the tank halts and fires.

If crewed by equally competent troops, NATO tanks hold a distinct technical advantage over Warsaw Pact tanks. Whether a single NATO tank in conjunction with NATO anti-tank missile defences can in reality hold off three times its number is a question which hopefully will never have to be answered.

The actual combat capabilities of Soviet tanks is hard to evaluate, because the different circumstances in which they have seen action do not bear comparison with what might occur in Central Europe. So far, Soviet equipment has been used most extensively in the Middle East conflicts of 1967 and 1973, with T-54s, T-55s and T-62s pitted against Centurions, M-48s, M-60s and even old Shermans. In both wars, the tank crews of Israel's Army scored impressive 'kill' ratios against Arab-manned Soviet tanks. In some cases, obsolete Shermans outfought T-55s. The reasons for this situation lie as much in the exceptional quality of the Israeli crews as in their equipment. It is worth noting that, in 1967, the Israeli Army savaged the Western-trained Jordanian Army, which used much the same equipment as the Israelis themselves. However, a confrontation between NATO and the Warsaw Pact is unlikely to find so great a discrepancy in crew competence as between the Arabs and the Israelis.

APPROXIMATE PROBABILITY OF 'KILLING' A TANK IF IT IS HIT

Soviet Weapon:	Range		PH/K*
T-62 BR-6:	1,641yds	(1,500m)	71 per cent
T-62 BK-6:	1,641yds	(1,500m)	75 per cent
Snapper:	2,735yds	(2,500m)	67 per cent
Swatter:	3,830yds	(3,500m)	67 per cent
Sagger:	3,282yds	(3,000m)	69 per cent
RPG-7:	328yds	(300m)	40 per cent

*Probability of a 'kill' if hit.

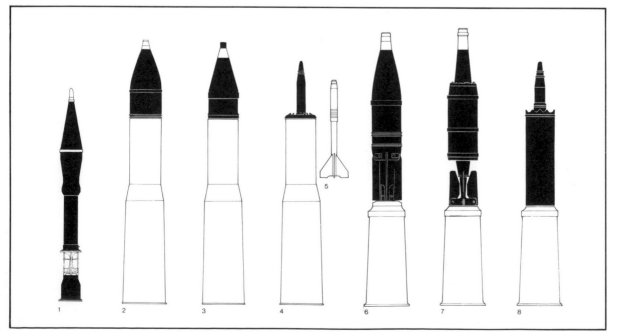

Left: 1. PG-9 round as used in the 2A28 gun of the BMP and SPG-9 recoilless gun. The small charge at the base of the round kicks the projectile out of the barrel at which time the rocket motor starts.
2. OF-18 high explosive-fragmentation, 115mm as is used in the U-5T gun of the T-62.
3. BK-6 high explosive, armour piercing, 115mm, shaped charge warhead, round as used in the U-5T gun of the T-62.
4. BR-6 armour piercing, fin-stabilized, discarding sabot, 115mm round as used in the U-5T gun of the T-62.
5. Tungsten carbide penetrator of the BR-6 round.
6. 125mm high explosive-fragmentation, fin-stabilized round of the T-64 and T-72 tank. This round contains 542ml of explosive.
7. 125mm high explosive, armour piercing, fin-stabilized round using a shaped charge warhead; used by the T-64 and T-72.
8. 125mm armour piercing, fin-stabilized, discarding sabot round as used in the T-64 and T-72. The projectile itself is a small finned tungsten carbide penetrator as with the 115mm BR-6 round.

Infantry Combat Vehicles

The changes in battlefield conditions brought about by the successful use of tanks in the Second World War necessitated significant alterations in infantry tactics. Tank units alone have little staying power and must operate with infantry units. Once the tanks have pushed through enemy defences, infantry consolidates the gains and then exploits the advance. Throughout the war, the combatant powers experimented with various ratios of tank and infantry units within the armoured divisions until a useful mix was obtained. At the time, a major problem confronting tacticians was the mobility of infantry. On foot, infantry could not keep up with the tanks, but if the tanks slowed down to accommodate them, they lost a major tactical advantage. Therefore, some form of transport had to be provided for the foot soldiers. Ordinary trucks did not have adequate cross-country performance, and most specialized cross-country vehicles were too underpowered to be fitted with thin armour. The Wehrmacht and the US Army relied principally on thinly armoured half-tracks, such as the ubiquitous Hanomog Sd Kfz 251 and the M-3 half-track, and this type of armoured infantry transporter became the predominant type during the war years.

The Red Army made virtually no use of armoured troop transporters during the war years, apart from 3,340 American M3A1 Scout cars, 804 M2 and M5 half-tracks and British Bren carriers supplied through Lend-Lease. The reasons for this are simple to trace. The massive industrial losses suffered after the 1941 débâcle forced the Soviet automotive industry to shift its attention to tank and self-propelled gun production. The pre-war Automotive Factory Nr.1 in Gorkii (GAZ) drastically cut back its production of the GAZ-AA light truck in favour of light tanks and the SU-76. Wartime output of trucks and tractors was only a tiny fraction of peacetime production and, therefore, the development of a specialized infantry carrier was out of the question. Pre-war experiments with a troop-carrying version of the BA-10 armoured car, designated BA-22, were shelved for the duration.

There were never enough trucks to go around, even with the substantial inflow of nearly half a million Lend-Lease vehicles, and a rather haphazard arrangement was initiated in 1942 to provide some measure of mobility to the infantry in tank brigades. Hand-holds were welded on to the hulls and turrets of new tanks. Before a battle, a squad of men would clamber on to each tank, grip on to the hand-holds and hang on for dear life as the tank raced towards its objective. Needless to say, these 'tank desant', as they were called, were very vulnerable, both to the jarring motion of the tank and to hostile fire. They were subjected not only to the usual volume of machine-gun fire and artillery but were also sniped at by the anti-tank and tank gun fire that their host tank attracted. Sometimes, when air-burst rounds stripped away nearly all of the helpless infantry before the objective was reached, this led to a bloodbath. At other times, the enemy was overrun and his positions were left in a shambles with scores of Soviet infantrymen suddenly deposited in his midst. It could be crude and effective, or just plain crude and costly.

Below: During the Second World War, the most common form of infantry transporter was the half-track. Although the half-track fell out of favour in the post-war years, the Czechoslovak Army continued to produce the OT-810 in preference to the wheeled Soviet BTR-152. The OT-810 is a heavily modified derivative of the German Hanomog Sd Kfz 251 Ausf D, which was manufactured in occupied Czechoslovakia during the war years. This photograph shows an OT-810, in the colourful five-tone summer camouflage pattern, being used by Czechoslovak forces during the Warsaw Pact manoeuvres conducted in the Doupov region of western Bohemia in June 1968, two months before the invasion of Czechoslovakia. (Eastfoto)

The BTR-152

In the last year of the war, the Red Army began designing a number of troop transporters. The first of these was the BA-64 Desantni based on the tiny BA-64 wheeled scout car. It was simply too small to be effective, though some were used as staff cars. The Moscow-based ZIS factory began development of a larger vehicle around its new ZIS-150/151 series of 2½-tonne trucks. It was given the subsequent factory serial number of —152, and the prefix BTR for BroneTransporteR, or armoured transporter. The first BTR-152 prototype was completed in 1946, but production was initially slow because of design short-comings and the diversion of ZIS attention to the needs of post-war recovery. Further work led to the BTR-152 V1, which entered series production in 1950. The BTR-152 V1 was the first mass produced Soviet troop carrier, and was based on the ZIS-157. Its armoured shape was vaguely related to both the Sd Kfz 247 and the M-3, but it was completely wheeled. Unlike the truck on which it was based, it had single tyres at the rear, but these had a wider tread and were connected to an external tyre pressure regulation system that allowed the driver to alter pressure to suit conditions. It carried a two-man crew and up to nineteen fully equipped soldiers. No overhead armour was provided and the side armour was no thicker than ½in (13mm). Usually, a single machine-gun was fitted for protection, the most common type being the 7.62mm Goryunov. Three firing ports were provided on either side

of the vehicle, with an additional pair at the rear. The exit was at the rear or over the side.

The decision by Soviet Ground Forces to adopt a wheeled transporter when most other nations were adopting superior tracked carriers was primarily due to economic reasons. At the time, the Soviet Union could not afford to mechanize its armoured infantry, to say nothing of its regular infantry divisions, with expensive tracked transporters. The performance of the BTR-152 was adequate enough until better equipment could be procured.

Two subsequent versions of the basic BTR-152 were to follow on the assembly lines: the BTR-152 V2, which dispensed with the external tyre regulation air pressure lines and the front power winch; and the BTR-152 V3, which reintroduced the winch and was fitted with an infra-red driving light and sighting devices.

Three major modified versions of the BTR-152 were also produced. The BTR-152K was essentially a BTR-152 V3 with an armoured roof cover, often used as a radio communications or special role vehicle. A custom-designed command version, the BTR-152U, was also series-produced. This was fitted with a much higher super-structure to allow the crew to stand within the armoured body. The final type, designated BTR-152A in the West, but in fact called the BTR-ZPU in the Soviet Union, mated a twin-barrelled KPV 14.5mm heavy anti-aircraft machine-gun in a ZPU-2-style mount to the basic BTR-152 chassis.

Left: Until mechanization of the infantry was complete, the Soviet Ground Forces relied on the old method of transporting some of the troops aboard tanks (tank desant). This photograph from the 1950s shows an infantry squad riding on a T-55. A pair of BTR-152 V2s can be seen in the background.

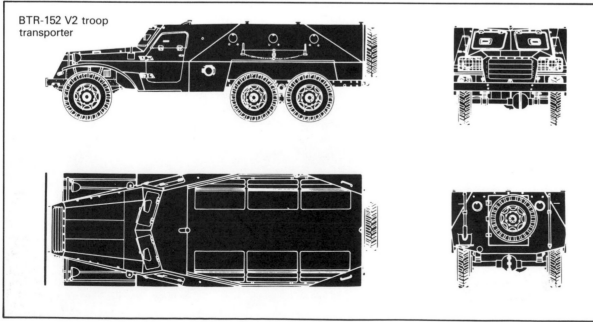

BTR-152 V2 troop transporter

The BTR-60

In the 1960s the majority of BTR-152 based vehicles were beginning to be withdrawn in favour of the newer BTR-60 series. Very few of the troop-carrying version are now in service in the Soviet Union, though a few remain in use among other Warsaw Pact countries, especially among the less favoured, such as Bulgaria and Romania. The BTR-152U is still in limited service, and some other BTR-152s are still used by engineer units to tow the PMR-3 and other minelaying devices.

At the same time that the BTR-152 V1 was being developed, a comparable vehicle based on the smaller GAZ-63 truck was also being worked on. This was known as the BTR-40. It was introduced in 1951 to complement the BTR-152 and was used mainly as a troop carrier and scout vehicle in reconnaissance companies and battalions. It could carry 10 men, counting its crew, and was usually armed with a single 7.62mm Goryunov machine-gun. An improved model with armoured roof, the BTR-40B, was eventually produced, and a chemical troops' model, the BTR-40khm with marking flag dispensers, was issued in small numbers. A version with a twin-barrelled 14.5mm KPV was also manufactured and, like the similar BTR-152 version, was also designated as the BTR-ZPU. The BTR-40 was replaced in its scouting role by the BRDM series (see p. 58) and is now not often seen, except in the Third World. The East German Army has given some of its old BTR-40s a new lease on life by equipping them with a Sagger anti-tank system similar to that on the BRDM.

In the 1960s, a more sophisticated family of second-generation troop carriers began to enter service. The BTR-60P was first issued to troops in 1961, to replace the old BTR-152. It had a smaller crew compartment than the BTR-152 but was fully amphibious. Water was drawn in underneath the vehicle and expelled by a propeller-driven water jet. Although it shared the same features as the BTR-152 in being both open-topped and thinly armoured, the BTR-60P's hull had a far better ballistic shape. In 1964, a version with protective overhead armour was introduced, and called the BTR-60PA. Finally, the BTR-60PB was developed. This is fully enclosed and has a small turret mounting the 14.5mm KPV heavy machine-gun. Although the troop complement has been reduced, and now comprises 2 crew and 8 troops, it is currently the most widely used version of this vehicle. A Romanian-built version, the TAB-72, is basically the same as the BTR-60PB but has new optical equipment on the left side of the turret. The BTR-60PB is still the most common armoured troop carrier in Soviet and Warsaw Pact motorized rifle divisions (except for Poland and Czechoslovakia), but it is gradually being replaced by the BMP and perhaps the MT-LB tracked transporter.

There is a whole new family of command vehicles based on the BTR-60P, collectively known as the BTR-60PU. These differ from one another in the types of radio gear carried and the stowage arrangement on the roof of the vehicle. One version, based on the BTR-60PB, has had its turret removed and plated over and a generator fitted above the old turret race. A clothes-line style antenna is fitted around the edge of the roof, and a high antenna can also be added to the array. A similar version retains the turret, but is unarmed. There is a forward air control version with a plexiglass port fitted to an unarmed turret and a high aerial at the rear. It is likely that these and subsequent radio and command versions will remain in service for a good many years.

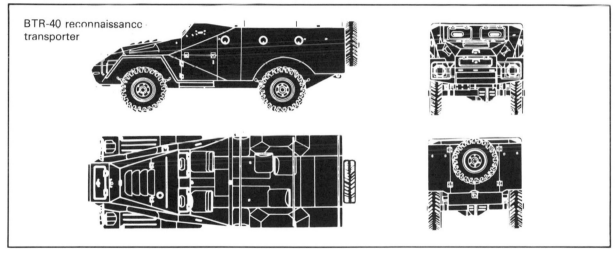

BTR-40 reconnaissance transporter

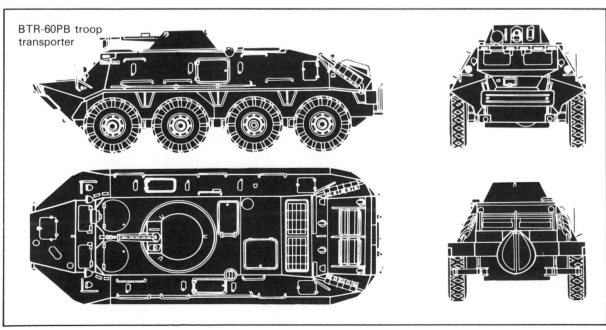

BTR-60PB troop transporter

Left: The BTR-152 was not a very sophisticated infantry transporter and was replaced by the BTR-60 family. This melodramatically staged photograph of a naval infantry landing in 1966 shows the BTR-60P, which was an early open-topped version of the BTR-60. The colonel in the foreground is armed with a PM Makarov pistol, while the marines all have AK-47s. In the background is another BTR-60P and a PT-76. (Sovfoto)

Below: A company of BTR-60Ps of the Soviet Naval Infantry swim ashore from *Alligator* Class tank landing ships during the Yug exercises in 1971. These vehicles have the new two-tone disruptive camouflage scheme common to the naval infantry, and carry the white band exercise markings. (Sovfoto)

Right, top and bottom: T-62A medium tanks. (US Army)

Right: The BTR-60P was followed by a fully enclosed version, the BTR-60PA. Many of these were replaced by the turretted BTR-60PB, and the vehicles turned over to non-infantry units for liaison and command duties. This particular BTR-60PA has been converted into a BTR-60PU command vehicle. It is being used by the commander of a BM-21 multiple rocket launcher battery in the Zabaikalski Military District in November, 1974. The vehicle is fitted with a mounting lug for the DS-0.9 stereoscopic rangefinder and a carrying case for it on the hull roof. Its tripod is stored on the fender, behind it is a PAB-2 periscopic artillery compass. Even when all this gear is stowed inside, the fact that the vehicle is a BTR-60PU command version can be determined by the multiplicity of radio aerials on the starboard side of the hull. (Sovfoto)

Right: The BTR-60PB is similar to the BTR-60PA, but is fitted with a small turret armed with a 14.5mm KPVT heavy machine-gun. (US Army)

Right: This interior view looking forward shows the cramped space in the BTR-60PB, even with the central benches and turret gunner's seat removed.

Left, top: A close-up of the Dushka mount on a T-62A. (US Army)
Left, bottom: A PT-76 amphibious reconnaissance tank. (US Army)

One of the principal tactical disadvantages of the BTR-60 series is its poor provision for troop exit. All of the exit ports are either on the roof or on the sides, which leave the departing troops extremely vulnerable to hostile fire. There is no turret roof hatch.

It was not surprising, therefore, that the Czechoslovak and Polish armies welcomed the opportunity to develop their own version of the BTR-60. This was one of the rare occasions when the Russians consented to the development of an armoured vehicle outside the Soviet Union by a Warsaw Pact country. While at first it might seem an unwarranted violation of the Warsaw Pact's commonality dogma, the matter is not as simple as that. The design was originated to take advantage of commonly available civil truck parts, and the armament, sights and many other features are compatible or identical to those used on the Soviet-built vehicle.

The SKOT (OT-64)

In 1959, the Czechoslovaks completed the initial set of plans for their transporter, which was to be built around the Tatra 928 engine. It was called SKOT (Stredni kolovy obrneny transporter, or medium armoured wheeled transporter). The prototype was completed in 1961 and, that year, Poland expressed interest in participating in the test and development programme. Joint production was eventually undertaken, and the new vehicle was first publicly displayed in Warsaw in 1964 at the 22 July Liberation Day Parade. The initial version, called simply SKOT or OT-64, had, in most respects, comparable or superior performance to the BTR-60. SKOT, too, is fully amphibious, but uses conventional propellers rather than a water jet. It has large doors for exit at the rear.

There was some interest in providing the SKOT with armament comparable to the BTR-60PB and while development continued, the Poles fitted many of their vehicles with a Goryunov or DShK machine-gun behind a large shield. These were designated SKOT-2, though in the West they are often called OT-64B. In 1964, an adaption was developed to mount the same turret, with the KPVT 14.5mm AA machine-gun, as that on the BTR-60PB. A riser was fitted at the base of the turret so that the gun would clear the forward hatches and other obstructions. This version was designated SKOT-2A. In 1964, the Military Technical Academy (WAT) in Warsaw developed an improved turret, which allowed the main gun to be elevated almost vertically for anti-aircraft fire. This version entered service as SKOT-2AP. Some of the original unarmed SKOTs are occasionally fitted with Sagger anti-tank missile man-packs on their rear decks to provide a measure of anti-tank protection.

Besides the basic troop transport version, there is a whole family of command, radio and repair vehicles based on the chassis. Of these, the most important are the R-2

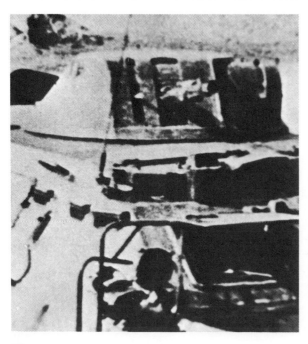

Left: This BTR-60PB of the Finnish Army clearly shows the rear engine deck area. Exit from the BTR-60PB is through the two roof hatches and two other small doors in the hull side. The awkward arrangement of the exit doors was a major factor in the decision of the Polish and Czechoslovak armies to independently develop their own transporter, the SKOT. (Kalevi Moilanen)

Opposite page, bottom left: The Romanians have introduced into military service at least two modified BTR-60s. The first, the TAB-72 (shown here), is basically a BTR-60PB with a new optical sight to the left of the turret mantlet. The other is a BTR 60PA, which has a 120mm mortar fitted amidships with armoured doors above it.

Opposite page, bottom right: The latest versions of the BTR-60PU, such as this one in service with the East German Army, have a railing-style aerial running along three sides, and a large 33ft. (10m) high radio mast to the right (not visible in this photograph). Extensive generator and transmitting gear is attached to the roof.

Right: The SKOT family was eventually fitted with the same type of 14.5mm gun turret as the BTR-60PB, but it was necessary to add a collar below it to clear the gun of the forward roof obstructions. This particular vehicle is unusual in that it has small vision ports along the sides of the collar. Recent models of the SKOT-2A (shown here) have a Sagger anti tank missile launcher on either side of the turret. Vehicles not in the Polish armoured divisions often do not carry the national insignia, but use registration codes instead. In the main, these codes begin with a two-letter suffix, usually beginning with the letter 'U'. The letter 'D' is also sometimes used. The white bison insignia visible on this vehicle is a regimental marking. (Eastfoto)

WHEELED TROOP TRANSPORTERS

	BTR-40	BTR-152 V3	BTR-60 PB	SKOT-2A
Derivative chassis:	GAZ-63A	ZIL-157	none	none
Crew/troop complement:	2/8	2/17	2/14	2/15
Weight:	5.3 tonnes	8.9 tonnes	10.3 tonnes	14.5 tonnes
Length:	18ft (5.5m)	22ft (6.8m)	25ft (7.6m)	24ft (7.4m)
Height:	6ft (1.8m)	6.5ft (2.0m)	7ft (2.3m)	9ft (2.7m)
Width:	6.25ft (1.9m)	7ft (2.3m)	7ft (2.3m)	8ft (2.5m)
Ground clearance:	10.875in (275mm)	11.625in (295mm)	18.75in (475mm)	16.125in (460mm)
Engine:	GAZ-40	ZIL-123	GAZ-49B	T 928-14
Horsepower:	80	110	90	180
Range:	177 miles (285km)	403 miles (650km)	310 miles (500km)	440 miles (710km)
Maximum speed:	50mph (80km/hr)	40mph (65km/hr)	50mph (80km/hr)	58mph (94km/hr)
Fording depth/ Speed in water:	35in (90cm)	35in (90cm)	amphibious 6mph (10km/hr)	amphibious 5.5mph (9km/hr)
Main armament:	7.62 CTME	7.02 CTME	14.5 KPVT	14.5 KPVT
NBC protection:	no	no	no	yes
Armour:	.375in (8mm)	.5in (12mm)	.55in (14mm)	.4in (10mm)

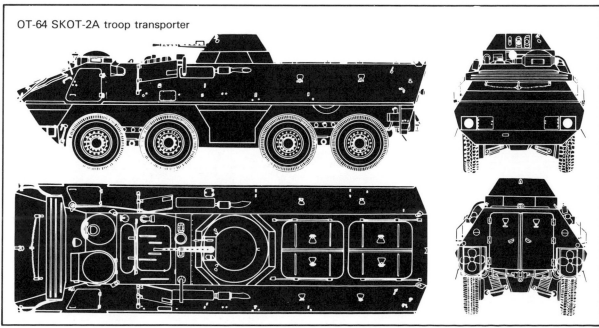

OT-64 SKOT-2A troop transporter

and R-3 radio command vehicles and the WPT-SKOT repair vehicle. These are either based on the initial SKOT type or on the SKOT-2A with the collar, but without the turret. The Czechoslovaks have produced an OT-64 with OT-65-style small turret fitted with an 82mm recoilless rifle. This has been exported to Morocco.

The SKOT is the principal wheeled transporter of the Czechoslovak and Polish armies, and it is occasionally used by Soviet forces during joint manoeuvres in Central Europe. It has been exported to several countries, including India, Uganda, and Morocco.

The BTR-50

At about the same time that the Soviet Ground Forces were receiving the new BTR-60, the first post-war tracked troop transporter, BTR-50P, was also entering service. The BTR-50P was intended to complement the BTR-60. But while the BTR-60 was destined to equip the motorized rifle divisions, the BTR-50 was geared for the mechanized infantry units within the armoured divisions.

The BTR-50P was a very simple conversion of the PT-76 amphibious scout tank. The forward area of the hull had a simple box structure added in place of the turret, and bench seats for 20 troops. It, too, is fully amphibious. The initial models were open topped, although, subsequently, a version with an armoured roof, the BTR-50PK, was developed. As in the case of the BTR-60, there is a whole family of related vehicles, including a number of command versions, designated BTR-50PU. These resemble the BTR-50PK but are distinguishable by their array of radio masts and power packs on the rear deck. The earliest types were simply conversions of the BTR-50PK, but more recent models have a new roof arrangement as well as double bays on the glacis plate on either side of the driver. The most recent version has a much higher roof than previous models and different types of stowage on the rear deck, including a large telescoping radio mast.

There are numerous minor derivatives of the BTR-50PK, including a transport model for mortars and recoilless rifles, repair vehicles, and a new engineer vehicle for launching a minefield-breeching rocket and tube. These differ from the basic model in their special stowage arrangement and specialized gear.

The BTR-50P is no longer in widespread use, and the BTR-50PK is gradually being phased out by the BMP and the MT-LB. The BTR-50PU will remain in use for many years.

The BTR-50 series has been widely exported and has seen action in both the Middle East and Indo-China. In Vietnam, some vehicles had a locally designed 14.5mm anti-aircraft semi-turret fitted on the rear deck.

The BTR-50 serves with all the Warsaw Pact armies except Czechoslovakia and Poland; both these countries use the Czech-manufactured version, the OT-62 TOPAS (Transporter Obojzivelay Pasovy Stredni, or medium tracked amphibian transporter). The basic OT-62 resembles the later production BTR-50PK, with double bays on the glacis plate, but has a more powerful engine. The TOPAS-2A has a small turret on the right bay, which carries a 7.62mm machine-gun inside and a T-21 82mm recoilless rifle externally. The TOPAS 2AP is fitted with the same WAT turret as the SKOT 2AP. Apart from its larger engine, the OT-62 can be distinguished from the BTR-50 by its large side-exit doors.

There are a number of TOPAS derivatives, including the Polish WPT-TOPAS recovery vehicle, which has a winch and can be easily distinguished by the shielded machine-gun (similar to that on the SKOT 2) carried over the right bay; another version mounting the M-59A recoilless rifle; and a squad vehicle for mortar teams. TOPAS is currently used in Czech armoured and motorized rifle divisions, and in the Polish 7th Marine Division. It has been exported, and has seen action in the Middle East. Eventually, it will be replaced by the Soviet infantry combat vehicle (BMP or Bronevaya Maschina Piekhota).

The BMP

The BMP is one of the most revolutionary vehicles to have entered Soviet Ground Force service in the past decade. For the first time, the Soviet Army has a troop carrier that is comparable or superior to those used by NATO. Moreover,

Left: Though the earliest versions of the OT-64 SKOT were unarmed, the Polish Army quickly began adding a small shielded machine-gun above the central hatches. This SKOT-2 carries the old-style white eagle insignia. In the late 1960s, this national insignia was replaced by the 'szachownica' (diamond-shaped red and white insignia used by the Polish armed forces), which is similar to the one in use on Polish aircraft since the 1920s.

Left, centre: The Poles were not entirely satisfied with the BTR-60PB-style turret, and developed the WAT turret for the SKOT-2AP. This allows the gun to be elevated for anti-aircraft fire. Here, a group of Polish soldiers, including one paratrooper from the 6th Pomorska Paratroop Division, exchange cigarettes with a pair of Romanian soldiers during the 'Braterstwo Broni' exercises in 1976.

Left, bottom: There are at least two command versions of the SKOT, the R-2 and R-3. These vehicles, probably of the R-2 type, are based on the turretless SKOT-2A, and have extensive additional radio sets and provisions for the mounting of various types of radio masts.

Right, top: The BTR-50 is a simple conversion of the PT-76 scout tank. This vehicle is a BTR-50PK with overhead armour. It quickly replaced the unarmoured BTR-50PA. (US Army)

Right: The BTR-50PK's lack of internal space and few firing ports make it impossible for the vehicle's infantry squad to fight from within the protection of its armour. As a result, the infantry fights dismounted, and is provided with covering fire from the vehicle's 7.62mm machine-guns. The soldier in the foreground is armed with an AK-47, while the infantryman in the centre is aiming his RPG-7 grenade launcher. (Sovfoto)

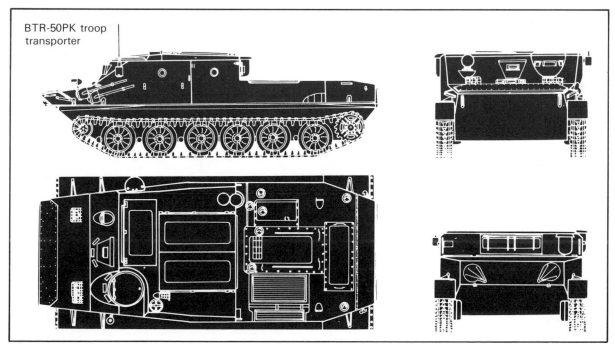

BTR-50PK troop transporter

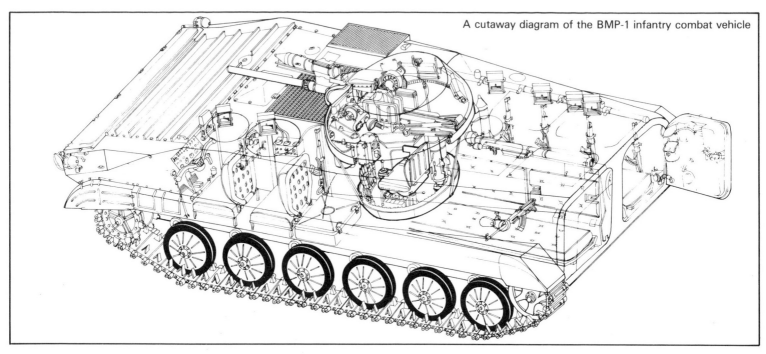

A cutaway diagram of the BMP-1 infantry combat vehicle

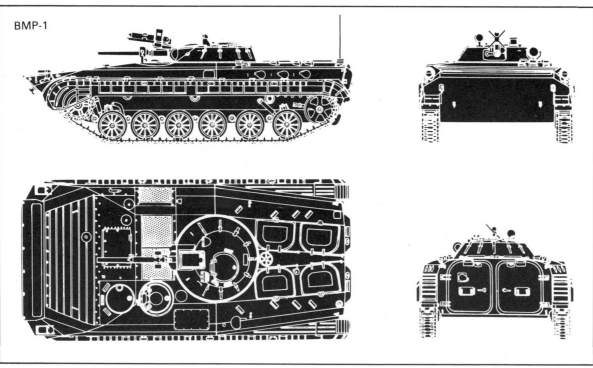

BMP-1

BMP-1
Weight: 13.9 tonnes
Crew: Driver plus 10 or 11 infantrymen
Length, overall: 22ft (6.74m)
Width: 9ft (2.9m)
Height: 6ft (1.9m)
Ground clearance:
15 ³/₈ in (390mm)
Fuel capacity:
Internal: 101 gallons (460 litres)
Fuel consumption:
Road: 3.1mpg (1.1 litres per km)
Swimming: .53mpg (1.5 litres per km)
Range: 310 miles (500km)
Maximum speed: 50mph (80km/hr); swimming 4-5mph
(7-8km/h) on water
Maximum gradient: 30°
Trench crossing: 6ft (2m)
Vertical obstruction: 32in (80cm)
Engine: V-6; 4 stroke diesel; liquid-cooled; 300hp at
2,600rpm; engine life approx. 500 hours

Armament:
Main gun: 73mm 2A28 low-pressure anti-tank gun,
unstabilized, elevation —4° to 33°, automatically
loaded, sustained rate of fire 8rpm
Ammunition stowed: 40 rounds, PG-9
Armour penetration: PG-9 fired between 800-3,000m
(875-3,283yds) at 0° 15¾in (400mm)
Supplementary armament: 9M14M Sagger (Malyutka)
anti-tank missile, 4-5 rounds stowed; coaxial 7.62mm
PKT; 250rpm; 2,000 rounds stowed; effective range
1,094yds (1,000m)
Fire control and vehicle vision devices:
Driver: Night infra-red, 55-66yds (50-60m) with infra-
red source
Commander: TPN 170 day sight, infra-red as per driver
Gunner: TPN 170 vision device, 1PN22M1 gun sight,
×6 magnification, 15° field of view during day. Night
operation on ambient light intensification 6° field of
view, range of 438-985yds (400-900m), × 6.7 magnification
Armour: ½in (14mm)

Below, right: The initial version of the BMP was not fitted with an NBC filtration system. This is evident by the absence of a port to the left of the turret. The PKM port on the BMP is the same as the three rear AKMS ports at the rear, while on the BMP-1 it is squarish. There is no circular snorkel cover behind the turret and the exit hatches on the rear hull roof are parallel to one another. These BMP belong to the Tashkent military school, and are shown here participating in manoeuvres in 1975. The light at the turret rear is a position light for night driving, and enables any vehicle following to keep track of the vehicle in front. Note that each squad member has a peri-scopic sight to aim his automatic rifle. (Sovfoto)

Bottom: The BMP-1 can propel itself across rivers by using its tracks. These BMP-1s belong to the mechanized infantry of a Soviet armoured division. They are shown here taking part in the Brotherhood of Arms manoeuvres in Poland in September 1976. While the external differences between the BMP and BMP-1 are slight, they can be seen in this photograph. The BMP-1 has a larger bow deflection plate, which on this vehicle has been raised for river-crossing. The additional rocker arm behind the first road wheel is also evident. The squarish PKM port is barely discernible, because the vehicle's company insignia (a white square, to the right of the number) has been painted on it. The edge of the inspection panel is noticeable above the '789' hull number. Note also that, during river crossings, the driver's forwardmost periscope can be raised to peer over the water deflection plate. (Sovfoto)

the BMP represents a fundamental shift in Soviet notions of combined infantry-tank operations.

Over the past two decades, military tacticians have been debating the pros and cons of current armoured troop transporters. Most of those in use with NATO, such as the FV 432, M113 and AMX-VTT, and those of the Warsaw Pact, such as the BTR-50 and BTR-60, belong to the so-called 'battlefield taxi' school of thought. Infantry squads use these vehicles to get as close as possible to their objective, and then dismount to carry out the attack on foot. The mechanized infantry in the vehicles could fire from the vehicle itself, but most of these transporters are ill-suited for this role. Only a small proportion of the troops could use their weapons at any one time, and they would have to reveal themselves to do so.

The new generation of troop carriers, which are referred to as infantry combat vehicles, differ from the earlier armoured troop transports in several key areas. In the first place, each vehicle is designed to allow the infantry squad to use their own weapons while sitting within the protective armour of the vehicle. Secondly, most of these vehicles are heavily armed to provide fire support for the infantry squad. These new designs allow the infantry to fight mounted or dismounted and, in fact, the new infantry tactics evoke memories of cavalry tactics.

The initial version of the Soviet infantry combat vehicle, or BMP, entered service in 1967. It carries a driver and a ten- or eleven-man squad and is fully amphibious. It is fitted with a combination gun mount consisting of a unique low pressure 73mm anti-tank gun for close-range fighting and a wire-guided 9M14M Sagger anti-tank missile launcher for long-range engagements. It is capable of 40 mph (65 km/hr) on roads and, in fact, is more mobile than either the T-55 or T-62. Its mobility advantage was one of the primary factors that prompted development of the new generation of T-64/72 tanks. In 1970, the BMP was succeeded by an improved model, the BMP-1, which is sometimes called the BMP-A in the West. Among the most important changes in the BMP-1 was the fitting of an NBC air filtration system.

The filtration system may prove to be an extremely important part of the BMP-1. Although both NATO and the Warsaw Pact armies have professed their unwillingness to use airborne contaminants, both sides have a sophisticated and varied array of weapon systems capable of doing so.

In the event of such an exchange taking place, conventional infantry, and infantry in unprotected transporters, could be rendered useless. Unlike the situation in 1915-18, when the gases had to be inhaled to debilitate, current biological and chemical agents can act very quickly through the skin. To guard against such agents, protective suits must be worn. However, many of these gases work so swiftly that troops would be obliged to be suited-up before the agents struck. This is impracticable since current suits are cumbersome and have serious drawbacks. Most are simply rubberized fabric, which ably protects

against outside contaminants, but at the same time keeps perspiration from evaporating properly. As a result, the users' body temperature soon rises, causing exhaustion or even heat-stroke. New suits that will be useful for more than a few hours are being developed, but they are not in widespread use.

Most of the current generation of infantry fighting vehicles like the BMP-1 are fully protected against chemical and biological agents. When a contaminated zone is reached, a built-in sensor system triggers an alarm and activates the system. Hatches are sealed and a slight over-pressure is built up inside the vehicle to prevent outside air from leaking in through any remaining cracks. The vehicle has a filtration system to purify air for the crew.

A number of small details distinguish the newer BMP-1 with the NBC gear from the earlier BMP. The filtration system itself is stored under a square hatch to the left of the main turret. The new BMP-1 has a different style of bow splash shield, and the fender pattern is different in a number of details. There is no rear fender tool box as there was on the BMP, and the roof exit hatches at the rear have been removed to form a shallow 'V' to accommodate the new round snorkel immediately behind the turret. The snorkel is used to provide an air source free from random splashes of water and surf. The BMP-1 entered service in East Germany and Poland in 1970 and is now in production in Czechoslovakia. It is called the BVP by the Czechs and BWP by the Poles.

In view of the considerable impact the BMP has had on the tactical doctrine of the Soviet Ground Forces, it is worth an especially detailed examination.

The BMP-1 is a 13.6-tonne vehicle powered by a 300hp diesel engine. Both the engine and transmission are located in the forward and forward right-hand portion of the hull, thereby protecting the rear crew compartment from forward hits. The driver is seated in the left forward portion of the hull, and steers the vehicle with a pneumatically-boosted yoke. He is provided with infra-red vision devices for night operations. The squad commander sits immediately behind the driver and has his own set of viewing instruments, including an infra-red searchlight. To his right, in the centre of the vehicle, is the turret with the main gun, a 73mm 2A28 smoothbore low-pressure gun with a 9M14M (NATO code-name, Sagger) wire guided anti-tank missile mounted directly above it. Behind the turret, in the rear of the vehicle, sit 8 troopers, with their backs toward each other, facing outward. Between the two rows is the main fuel cell, and there are two additional fuel cells located within the two rear doors. There are an additional four large rectangular hatches in the roof above them. Each trooper has a firing port and a viewing periscope. The two forwardmost ports are used by the two-squad PKM machine gunners, and the remaining ports are adapted to fit the barrels of the squad's AKMS-type assault rifles. The two troopers at the vehicle's rear are provided with an additional port to cover the rear. There are brackets for the SA-7 Grail, even though not all BMPs carry this weapon.

There is considerable debate within NATO regarding which class of weapon would be most useful as the supplementary squad support gun. Some advocate using an anti-tank weapon, others an anti-helicopter weapon, and others, a dual-purpose weapon. Soviet designers have leaned heavily in favour of an anti-tank weapon. There were enormous technical problems inherent in this decision, but they have been overcome in a very clever manner. Even a small and relatively ineffective rifled anti-tank gun, such as the D-56T 76mm gun used on the PT-76, is too large and heavy to fit on a troop carrier, and a recoilless rifle or other rocket weapon has the problem of backblast. The 2A28 is a unique cross between a conventional gun and a rocket weapon. It consists of a simple tube launcher and a PG-9 round that is very similar to that used in the RPG-7 anti-tank weapon. The PG-9 is fitted with a small charge that blows it clear of the gun tube, at which point the rocket motor cuts in and boosts the speed. The round leaves the barrel at 438yd/sec (400m/sec) and, once the motor starts, this increases to 740yd/sec (665m/sec). Once the PG-9 is free of the tube, its fins deploy to give the round stability. The PG-9 round is capable of penetrating 11¾in (300mm) of armour set at 90° at any range and, therefore, is fully capable of piercing

Left: Many BMP-1s are being equipped with a new version of the Sagger missile fitted with semi-automatic guidance identical to this one. This greatly improves the chance for a first round hit and eases the task of the gunner.

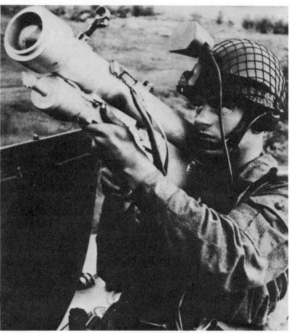

Left: Every third BMP carries an SA-7 Grail anti-aircraft missile, which can be fired from outside the top roof hatch. This is the latest version of the SA-7, called the SA-7b. Note the IFF (identification friend or foe) equipment fitted to this Polish soldier's helmet.

Left: The BMP-R is a new recon-naissance version of the BMP-1. This grainy shot from *Red Star* is one of the only unclassified photographs of it.

Due to the inaccuracy of the 2A28 beyond 1,400yds (1,300m), the BMP is fitted with a 9M14M Malyutka ('Little One') anti-tank rocket launcher. The Malyutka is a first-generation wire guided anti-tank missile and, to be effective, requires a very highly skilled gunner. The gunner controls the missile by using a small joystick that pops up from beneath his seat. He must keep track of both the missile and the target, which is no mean feat. The 9M14M's shaped charge warhead can penetrate up to 15¾ in (400mm) of conventional steel armour. It is estimated that, at 1,000yds (1km) and beyond, a well-trained Malyutka gunner has a 61 per cent chance of hitting a fully exposed tank whether stationary or moving, whereas he has only a 31 per cent chance against a tank in hull defilade. The Malyutka is ineffective at close ranges, since the gunner requires a few seconds to gain control of the rocket once it has been launched. It is also ineffective beyond 3,250yds (3km), as the wire spool runs out.

As with the 2A28 gun, the BMP must be stationary for the 9M14M to be fired accurately. Four additional rounds are carried, two in the right of the turret, and two more in the right of the hull near the right side of the PKM machine gunner. A 9M14M takes 27 seconds to fly 3,250yds (3km), which is approx. 131yds per sec (120m/sec), and about 45 to 50 seconds to load. The gunner reloads the round by opening a small roof hatch and guiding the new round down a tracked cradle. Once in place, the gunner must fiddle around with a small stick to fold out the stabilizing fins. Unfortunately, this breaks up the air filtration seal.

This cumbersome loading procedure means that the 9M14M can only be fired at a rate of about one every two minutes. Moreoever, it is a rather slow projectile and can be seen in flight. This can work to the advantage of the BMP gunner, since he can switch targets in mid-flight. On the other hand, if a Sagger is spotted early enough, an opposing tank fired on after crossing the crest of a hill need only back down the hill to avoid the missile. Unlike the main gun, the 9M14M has no night sighting equipment provided for it. This is mainly due to the fact that Soviet night sights, whether infra-red or starlight intensifiers, are only effective up to about 876yds (800m), while the Malyutka's effective range is far beyond that.

The 9M14M/2A28 combination gives the BMP complementary zones of fire from point-blank to 3,250yds (3km). The weapons are small, cheap and light and offer a clever solution to a very difficult technical problem. In contrast, NATO types like the Bundeswehr Marder use a 20mm

Top: The Mi-26 Hind-D assault helicopter is an airborne counter-part of the BMP-1. Like the BMP, it carries a small squad of 8 troops. It is armed with a four-barrel 23mm autocannon in the nose, and can carry a variety of other stores, including the UB-32 57mm rocket, the pads of which are evident on these Hind-Ds participating in the July 1977 Karpaty exercises. There are also launch racks, which are probably for the new generation AT-2b Swatter anti-tank missiles. The Hind-D will probably be used by the newly-forming Brigada Osobova Naznacheniya (BON) or Special Duties Airborne Brigades, which are designed to seize forward airfields and landing zones, carry out diversion attacks in the enemy's rear and attack crucial communication lines. (Sovfoto)

Above: The BMP-SON (designation uncertain) is an artillery radar vehicle used in conjunction with the new self-propelled 122mm and 152mm guns. (US Army)

virtually any tank now in service, with the possible exception of those with Chobham armour. The 2A28 is supplemented by a PKT 7.62mm coaxial machine-gun.

The 2A28 weighs a remarkably light 254lb (115kg), which has allowed the designers to incorporate a simple automatic loading system. Forty rounds are stowed in a circular clip at the base of the turret floor. An electrically driven loader rotates the clip until a round is located, grasps the round, elevates the gun to gain clearance, rams the round home, and repositions itself for the next circuit. The autoloader gives the BMP a rather high rate of fire of about 8 rounds per minute, but the need to elevate the gun for each loading detracts from its overall performance, since the gunner cannot use the previous shot to adjust his second.

The 2A28 is very accurate when fired from a stationary vehicle, but as it has no stabilization system it is incapable of firing accurately on the move. Even up to 875yds (800m), the 2A28 has a 50 per cent chance of hitting a stationary tank, in spite of its crude stadiametric ranging reticle. The gun is ineffective beyond 1,400yds (1,300m), and is less effective against a moving target or one in hull defilade. The gun's most serious drawback is that the rounds are badly disturbed by cross-wind; a problem that is shared by the RPG-7 rounds. They tend to fly into the wind and unless the gunner can estimate the wind drift, his aim will be badly upset.

The gun has a blind spot in the 10 o'clock to 11 o'clock position due to the obstruction of the commander's infra-red searchlight. Therefore, it can only be depressed 5°, which limits the vehicle's ability to fire from a hull defilade position.

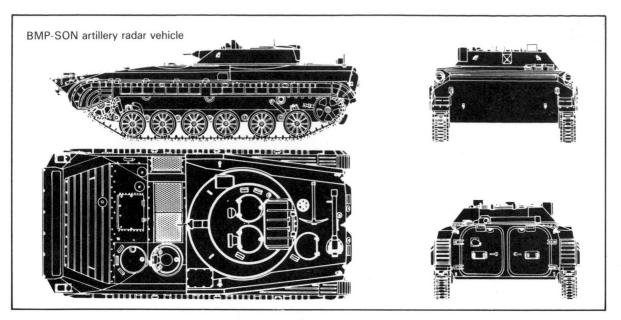

BMP-SON artillery radar vehicle

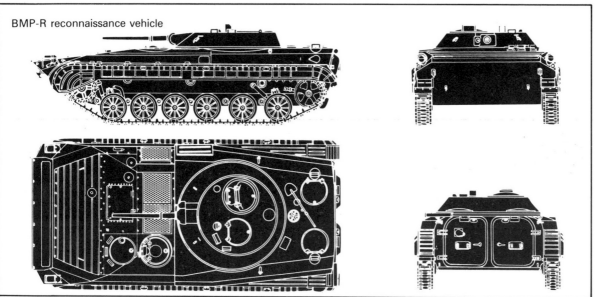

BMP-R reconnaissance vehicle

autocannon, which is very effective against thinly armoured troop carriers (such as the BMP) over a range of 3,250yds (3km), but are virtually useless against tanks.

A BMP-equipped motorized rifle company consists of 108 troops in 10 BMPs. There are 3 platoons, each with 3 BMPs, and there is a single headquarters/command BMP. Each platoon has 3 squads, totalling 32 men, in 3 vehicles. The first and third squads have 11 men, while the second has 10. All vehicles have at least 6 or 7 AKMS assault rifles, 2 PKM machine-guns, an RPG-7 and pistol armament for the driver and commander. In the first and third squads there may be an SA-7 Grail anti-aircraft rocket launcher and crew and the first squad may also be equipped with an SVD sniper rifle.

The BMP's thin armour, which does not exceed ½in (14mm), leaves it vulnerable to a wide variety of anti-tank weapons. While the front armour is very well sloped, a hit from any conventional tank gun will penetrate and probably hit the transmission, engine or driver, thus immobilizing the vehicle. It is especially vulnerable to flank attacks and, in fact, at ranges under 219yds (200m), an ordinary .50 calibre machine-gun firing AP rounds will penetrate the armour. A hit under the turret area is likely to result in the detonation of the PG-7 rounds or Saggers, leading to a catastrophic explosion. At 1,642yds (1,500m), the standard NATO 105mm gun and fire control system with APDS ammunition has a 50 per cent chance of a first round hit. This same probability also applies when using a HEAT round at 1,300yds (1,200m). The optically guided TOW anti-tank missile is given a 50 per cent chance up to 3,282yds (3km) and the Dragon 50 per cent up to 1,094yds

(1km). The small LAW has a 50 per cent chance at 164yds (150m). On receiving a solid hit from nearly any of these projectiles, the vehicle would be either immobilized or destroyed. The BMP's light armour also makes it very susceptible to mines.

The Soviet Ground Forces have always stressed the use of related vehicle chassis for special-purpose roles, and it comes as no surprise that a whole family of BMP derivatives is beginning to appear in the Soviet press. A new enlarged turret version of the BMP-1, apparently designated BMP-R, was shown for the first time in a 1978 issue of *Red Star*. The BMP-R uses the same hull as the BMP-1 but, due to the use of a larger two-man turret, carries far fewer troops and has only two small circular hatches behind the main turret in place of the usual four large hatches. This would seem to indicate that the crew comprises roughly six men. The BMP-R is a reconnaissance version, probably intended to replace the PT-76. Another command derivative, probably designated BMP-Sh, also uses a modified BMP-1 chassis with a small turret and extensive radio gear. This version carries only a small machine-gun in the turret and has a modified rear deck and fewer crew.

A radar direction-finder version of the BMP-R is also in service with the new 122mm and 152mm self-propelled gun batteries. It uses the same large turret as the BMP-R, but is only machine-gun armed. A rectangular folding radar, probably for target acquisition, is mounted at the rear of the turret. This vehicle may be designated BMP-SON.

The reception of the BMP-1 within the Soviet Ground Forces has not been uniformly enthusiastic, for the vehicle

TRACKED TROOP TRANSPORTERS

	BTR-50P	OT-62 TOPAS 2	MT-LB
Derivative chassis:	PT-76	PT-76	MT-L
Crew/troop complement:	2/20	2/18	2/11
Weight:	14 tonnes	15 tonnes	9.7 tonnes
Length:	22ft (6.7m)	23ft (7.0m)	21ft (6.4m)
Height:	6ft (1.8m)	7ft (2.1m)	6ft (1.8m)
Width:	10.5ft (3.2m)	10ft (3.1m)	9ft (2.8m)
Ground clearance:	14.5in (370mm)	14.5in (370mm)	16.375in (415mm)
Engine:	V-6	PV-6	YaMZ-238V
Horsepower:	240	300	240
Range:	161 miles (260km)	155 miles (250km)	310 miles (500km)
Maximum speed:	28mph (45km/hr)	37mph (60km/hr)	38mph (61km/hr)
Swimming speed:	9mph (15km/hr)	7mph (11km/hr)	3-4mph (5-6km/hr)
Main armament:	7.62mm CTME	T-21 82mm	7.62mm PKT
NBC protection:	no	yes	yes
Armour:	.6in (15mm)	.75in (20mm)	.55in (14mm)

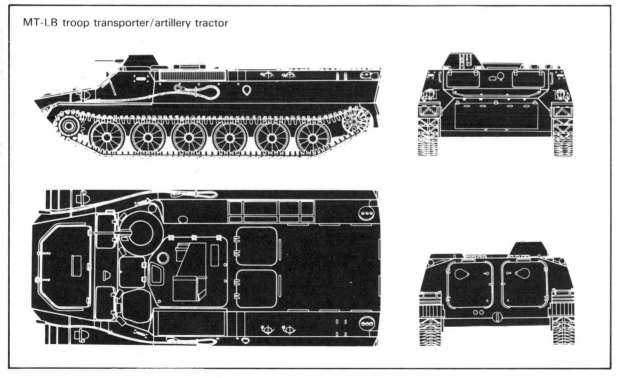

MT-LB troop transporter/artillery tractor

is somewhat controversial due to its high cost and complexity. Also, its revolutionary influence on infantry tactics has prompted some of the more traditional officers to question its real fighting value. At about the same time that the BMP entered service, another more conventional transporter appeared, the MT-LB, which may have been an 'insurance policy' in the event of the BMP being unsuccessful.

The MT-LB
The MT-LB is a derivative of the new MT-L towing tractor family that will eventually replace the GT-T family. Destined primarily for use in the Arctic, the MT-L is an unarmoured tractor made of ductile aluminium. The MT-LB is a lightly armoured, very low-slung version capable of carrying twelve troops in its rear compartment.

It has a small machine-gun cupola at the right front corner adjacent to the driver's station. When fitted with special wide grouser tracks, the MT-LB is designated MT-LBV.

Until now, most photographs have shown the MT-LB in use as an artillery tractor. However, recently, photographs showing it being used as an infantry troop transporter have appeared. It has excellent performance in snow and will probably be employed in sub-Arctic areas or by units, such as engineer units, that do not require the BMP's fighting characteristics. Should the BMP prove too expensive, some Category II or Category III units might receive the MT-LB in place of the BMP. Several MT-LB derivatives have been reported, including at least three artillery command vehicles and an artillery-related radar vehicle with a large rear-mounted superstructure or turret, possibly designated MT-SON.

Above: Initially the MT-LB was believed to be primarily an artillery tractor, but photographs such as this, taken during the June 1976 Sever exercises, clearly indicate its additional use as a troop transporter. These two vehicles are modernized improvements of the BTR-50, and the infantry they carry must fight dismounted. (Sovfoto)

Centre: The MT-LB has only a single firing port on the left side and so cannot be employed in the same fashion as the BMP-1. Its similarity to many of the new generation of armoured vehicles, such as the 122mm self-propelled howitzer, is quite striking, and highlights the great emphasis Soviet military designers place on commonality of parts. (US Army)

Bottom: The K-63 is a PT-76 derived armoured troop transporter developed by the People's Republic of China. It is small and cramped and quite simple, even by Soviet standards. Small numbers, such as this one captured by troops belonging to the Army of the Republic of Vietnam, saw action in Vietnam. (US Army)

Airborne Combat Vehicles

The Red Army was for a long time one of the most enthusiastic proponents of airborne forces. Correspondingly, they showed a great deal of interest in the development of air transportable vehicles for airborne support. The Soviet Army today is the only armed force to field significant numbers of air droppable armoured combat vehicles.

The bitter lessons of the costly paratroop battles at Viazma and on the Dnepr during the war prompted the development of a light air-droppable self-propelled gun to give the paratroops a measure of protection against opposing armour. Earlier paratroop vehicles such as the KT flying tank, the T-34 airborne tank and the Grokhovsky airbus did not fulfil these needs, and a wholly new vehicle, the ASU-57, was developed. This began entering service in the early 1950s.

The ASU-57

The ASU-57 bears more than a passing resemblance to the wartime OSU-76 self-propelled gun prototype and, in fact, the designs are probably related. It was designed with every possible weight-saving factor in mind, and was constructed using a mixture of steel and duraluminum. To keep the weight below four tonnes it was necessary to limit armour to the front and sides, and even that was kept to a paltry ¼ in (6mm). The top is completely open and the rear is aluminium. The armour provided is just barely adequate against shrapnel and low velocity infantry weapons. The engine is from the Pobeda passenger car, and the gun is a development of the wartime ZIS-2 anti-tank gun.

The ASU-57 was first publicly displayed in 1957. At the time, the delivery method was by means of a conventional array of heavy cargo parachutes. The ASU-57 was packed into a special P-90 aluminium parachute container. The P-90 was quite streamlined, but was rather small and the ASU-57's barrel protruded. One P-90 container could be slung underneath both wings of a TU-4 heavy bomber between the two engines. This gave the bomber the appearance of carrying two enormous gun pods under its

Below: The diminutive ASU-57 airborne tank destroyer is one of the few vehicles of its kind still in service. This vehicle, participating in the 1967 Dnepr manoeuvres, is an early production model. It has the Ch-51 gun with multi-slotted muzzle brake. When leaving the dropping zone, the crew has to avoid running over parachute shrouds. Otherwise, they risk badly fouling the vehicle's running gear. The white Soviet airborne forces insignia is prominently displayed above the gun. (Sovfoto)

ASU-57 assault gun

wings. In 1959, the heavy AN-12 transport was brought into service with the Soviet Air Force (Voyenno Vozdushnyye Sily), which allowed the Soviet Airborne Forces (Vozdushno Desantnÿe Voiska) to develop better dropping techniques.

A special transport pallet was designed and a new parachute technique was developed. Two ASU-57s on their special pallets could be carried and, once over the target area, a special auxiliary drogue chute was deployed from the rear hatch, which when it opened, dragged out the pallet. Once free of the aircraft, a second series of drogue chutes opened to stabilize the platform and prevent it from tumbling. When stable, the main cargo chutes opened. These, by themselves, were not sufficient to land the vehicle safely. The usual landing speed of a paratrooper is about 15-16ft per second (4.5-5m/s), while a pallet with full cargo chutes falls at nearly 49ft per second (15m/s). However, there was a special retro-rocket charge underneath the pallet and a detonator for the retros dangled below the pallet. A few seconds before the pallet

was due to hit the ground, the detonator below would send up a signal to ignite the retros and slow down the pallet sufficiently. The pallet itself was designed to be collapsible and to absorb a good deal of the landing shock. The crew would jump separately and, once the vehicle and crew were reunited, the ASU-57 would be driven off the platform.

The ASU-57 is usually accompanied by a squad of paratroop riflemen who ride in the rear or on top of it. While in the landing zone, they make certain of preventing loose shroud lines from catching in the running gear of the ASU-57. This can be a serious problem. The pallet system allows the Soviet Airborne Forces to use far smaller parachutes than would otherwise be necessary.

The vehicle itself is crewed by three men: a driver, gunner and loader. It is a very simple vehicle with much of its fuel system, ammunition stowage and engine components exposed. This layout combined with the vehicle's thin armour, make it very vulnerable to hostile fire. Yet, keeping these limitations in mind, it is a useful vehicle.

Left: The ASU-57 is lashed to a special pallet for airdropping. To facilitate ground handling, the pallet has a pair of detachable wheels fitted. (Flight Plan)

Below: This standard production model of the ASU-57, seen here in January 1978 taking part in exercises, uses the Ch-51M gun with a conventional double-baffle muzzle brake. The troops jumping off the vehicle wearing mechanized force padded helmets and are armed with the new AKD 5.56mm paratroop assault rifle. The airborne insignia on this vehicle is the simplified silhouette style. (Sovfoto)

Right, top: A BTR-152 V2 troop transporter. (US Army)

Right, bottom: A BTR-50PK troop transporter. (US Army)

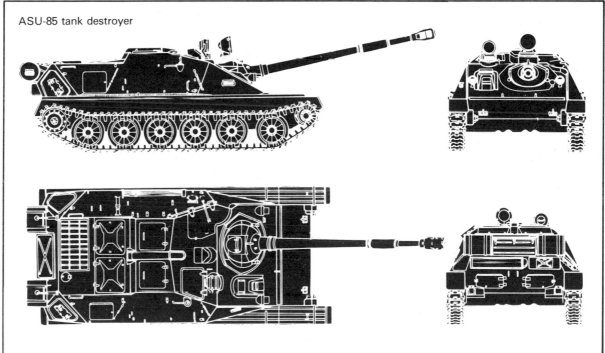

ASU-85 tank destroyer

Two models of the ASU-57 were produced: an initial production batch using the early Ch-51 gun with multi-slotted muzzle brake, and the standard production model with the Ch-51M and a conventional double-baffle muzzle brake. The ASU-57 formed the automotive basis for the AT-P artillery tractor, which is also air droppable.

Although the ASU-57 is still in use with the Airborne Forces, it is rapidly being phased out in favour of the far more sophisticated BMD 1 airborne combat vehicle. The ASU-57 was supplied in very small numbers to the Egyptian Army, and it saw some combat in 1967. It does not form a regular part of the Polish 6th Pomorska Airborne Division, as is so often reported, nor does it seem to have been distributed to any other Warsaw Pact countries.

The ASU-85

It was evident from the start that the ASU-57's anti-tank capabilities were, at best, marginal. As a result, work was initiated on a more heavily armed vehicle, the ASU-85, which was first publicly displayed in 1962. The ASU-85 is a member of the prolific PT-76 family. It is much more heavily armoured than other related types and has an effective 85mm gun. Its main drawback is its weight and lack of amphibious capability. It is too heavy and awkward to be parachuted, and so it must be airlifted in an AN-12 transport, which has to land on an airstrip. Therefore, the tactical utility of the ASU-85 is far more limited than the compact, but under-armed, ASU-57.

The ASU-85 is far more sophisticated than the ASU 57 and has infra-red night fighting equipment. Since 1973 some versions have also carried a retrofitted anti-aircraft machine-gun. The ASU-85 is used by the armoured battalions of the Soviet and Polish airborne divisions, but has not been exported beyond this. It is unclear what, if any, armoured equipment (apart from the SKOT) is used by the Czech airborne brigade. The ASU-85 does not appear to have seen any combat service, though some were dropped in Prague in 1968.

The ASU-57 and ASU-85 offer the Soviet Airborne Forces overlapping qualities, but neither vehicle by itself is really satisfactory in a sophisticated combat situation. The ASU-57 offers the tactical flexibility needed, and the ASU-85 offers the firepower, but both have corresponding disadvantages.

The BMD

In 1970, the Airborne Forces began to receive the BMD (Bronevaya Maschina Desantnaya) airborne combat vehicle, which has gone a long way towards remedying these deficiencies. The BMD is basically an airborne counterpart of the Soviet infantry's BMP, and uses the same turret and armament system. It has a new type of chassis that does not appear to be related to any previous sort. The BMD is smaller than the BMP, carries only a six-man squad, and is even more cramped. Two crewmen sit on either side of the driver, and the other four sit in the rear behind the turret. There are no firing ports in the rear as on the BMP, but there are two machine-gun ports at the front corners of the vehicle.

The BMD-1 constitutes a major step forward in airborne vehicles and is unique amongst the world's armies. With its anti-tank, amphibious, air-droppable and troop transport capabilities, the BMD seems ideally suited to the needs of airborne units. Paratroop forces can ill-afford a variety of vehicles to suit their needs, and to find a single vehicle with all these uses combined is a real blessing.

The BMD-1 is dropped with a pallet that is very similar to the one for the ASU-57 and, therefore, is much more useful than the older ASU-85. At the moment, it serves only with the Soviet Airborne Forces but, eventually, it will probably be supplied to Poland. Until then, the Polish 6th Pomorska Airborne Division will go on using BMPs which, unfortunately, have to be airlifted. Some recent films of BMD-1 drops from the new IL-76 transport have shown it without a pallet.

The ASU-57, ASU-85 and BMD-1 are the only custom-built airborne vehicles in service, but other Soviet vehicle types can be airlifted. The AN-12 can carry a diverse load up to 20 tonnes and can accommodate a PT-76, ZSU-23-4, Frog-4 and any number of smaller vehicles. The AN-22 Antei can carry up to 100 tonnes of equipment, and is, therefore, capable of hauling aloft virtually any current Soviet armoured vehicle. However, it must be kept in mind that to take advantage of these aircraft, the Soviet Airborne Forces would have to first seize an airstrip to land such equipment and, under tactical conditions such as those experienced during the Second World War, this would probably be impossible.

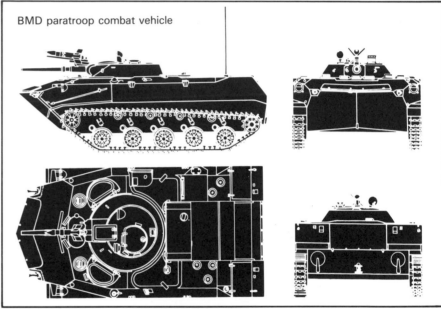

BMD paratroop combat vehicle

Left: The ASU-85 assault gun is a very effective tank destroyer, but is rather on the heavy side and cannot be parachuted. It is fitted with a full range of infra-red searchlights and sights for night combat. It is used primarily by the Soviet and Polish airborne forces. (Sovfoto)

Left, bottom: The tiny BMD paratroop combat vehicle is a reduced size BMP. It is crewed by a driver and gunner, and carries six paratroopers: four in the rear and two in the front beside the driver. This photograph, taken during a parade in Moscow in 1977, shows the different arrangement used for ceremonial occasions, with all six paratroops riding in the rear compartment. (US Army)

Below, right: This rather grainy shot shows two new versions of the BMD: an improved BMD with additional rear fuel cells and, in the background, a command BMD with additional radio equipment. The paratrooper in the foreground is armed with the new AKD assault rifle.

Bottom: This BMD on a training exercise in the Transcaucasus in 1974 has just cleared its landing pallet as other BMDs are air-dropped. (Sovfoto)

AIRBORNE VEHICLES

	ASU-57	ASU-85	BMD-1
Weight:	3.35 tonnes	14 tonnes	9.9 tonnes
Crew:	3	4	2/6
Length, overall:	16ft (5.0m)	27ft (8.5m)	17ft (5.3m)
Length of hull:	11ft (3.5m)	20ft (6.0m)	17ft (5.3m)
Width:	7ft (2.1m)	9ft (2.8m)	8.5ft (2.6m)
Height:	4ft (1.2m)	7ft (2.1m)	6ft (1.8m)
Ground clearance:	8in (204mm)	15.75in (400mm)	15.75in (400mm) variable
Engine:	M-20E	V-6	V-6
Horsepower:	55	240	280
Maximum speed:	28mph (45km/hr)	27mph (44km/hr)	50mph (80km/hr)
Range:	155 miles (250km)	161 miles (260km)	198 miles (320km)
Armour:	.25in (6mm)	1.5in (40mm)	.75in (20mm)
Main gun:	Ch-51M 57mm	D-5-S85 85mm	2A28 73mm
Penetration performance (at right-angles) at 1,000m (1,094 yds)	APHE: 3.375in (85mm) HVAP: 3.875in (100mm)	APHE: 4in (102mm) HVAP: 5.125in (130mm)	PG-9: 11.75in (300mm)
Rounds stowed:	30	40	40
Elevation:	−5 to +12°	−4 to +15°	−4 to +33°
Traverse:	22°	12°	360°
Secondary armament:	none	7.62mm PKT	Sagger 9M14M 3 x PK 7.62mm

Reconnaissance Vehicles

and Tank Destroyer Derivatives

During the Second World War, the Soviet Army made extensive use of both Lend-Lease M3A1 scout cars and BA-64 armoured cars for reconnaissance purposes. These supplemented Valentine and T-70 light tanks in the scouting role, and were also useful for liaison work, for transporting forward artillery observers and for moving small scouting parties. Both lingered on in service until they were eventually replaced in the early 1950s by the BTR-40.

The BRDM

The BTR-40 was not an unqualified success as a scout car. It was no worse than the M3A1, but it had no amphibious capability and so was restricted in performing its main mission. In 1957, a prototype of a new amphibious scout car was built, known as the BRDM (Bronirovannaya Razviedyvatielno Dozornaja Maschina or armoured scout vehicle). The BRDM is often erroneously referred to as the BTR-40P, which originates from its East German designation of SPW-40P, but the proper Soviet designation is simply BRDM. The BRDM corrected many of the deficiencies of the BTR-40. It has good all-terrain

performance, and has a set of flotation wheels at mid-section which can be lowered to clear obstructions or to lower the vehicle's overall ground pressure. Its water propulsion system was basically the same as on the PT-76 scout tank. While the pre-production series supposedly did not have an armoured roof, the standard production models did. Armament usually consisted of a single 7.62mm Goryunov machine-gun.

Besides providing 'eyes and ears' for headquarters, it was expected to serve as an NBC scout and so was usually provided with a DP Geiger counter and PKhR-54 chemical detector. Towards the end of production, some vehicles were fitted with a heavy KPVT or DShK machine-gun. The BRDM served primarily in the reconnaissance battalions of tank divisions.

There were two basic derivatives of the BRDM: the BRDM-U was a standard BRDM fitted with extra command radios; and BRDM-rkh was an NBC troop vehicle, fitted at the rear with marking flag dispensers. In the late 1950s, the Soviet development of wire guided anti-tank missiles culminated in the first service model, known in the West as the AT-1 Snapper and in the Warsaw Pact as the 3M6

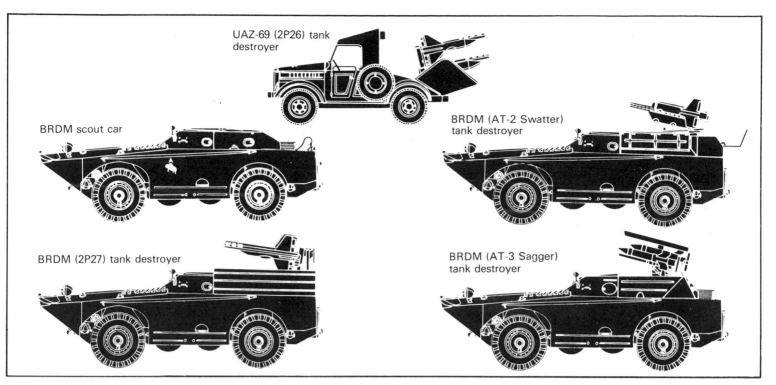

UAZ-69 (2P26) tank destroyer

BRDM scout car

BRDM (AT-2 Swatter) tank destroyer

BRDM (2P27) tank destroyer

BRDM (AT-3 Sagger) tank destroyer

Far left, upper: Two East German SK-1 armoured cars on patrol. This tiny 2-man vehicle was a counterpart to the Soviet BA-64B. It was produced in small numbers in 1949, mainly for use with the Volkspolizei (East German militia) and border patrols, and is now being phased out in favour of other equipment being withdrawn from regular Army service.

Far left, lower: The BTR-40 scout transporter bore more than a passing resemblance to the wartime Lend-Lease M3A1 scout car. It could be used to transport troops or scouting parties. A fully enclosed version, the BTR-40K, was also produced.

Near left, upper: This overhead view into a BTR-40 shows the seating arrangement and use of the firing ports. The size of the squad for the BTR-40 was usually somewhat greater than is indicated by this photograph. (Soviet Embassy via George Balin)

Near left, lower: Some old BTR-40s of the East German Army have been given a new lease on life by being rebuilt as tank destroyers equipped with a launch array for 9M14M Malyutka wire guided anti-tank missiles.

Top, right: The BRDM (2P27) equipped with the 3M6 (AT-1 Snapper) wire guided anti-tank missile was the first tank destroyer version of the BRDM to enter service.

Bottom, right: The BRDM (AT-2 Swatter) differed from the other anti-tank missiles by being radio guided. It is judged to be probably the most effective tank destroyer of the family, with an 85-90 per cent chance of a first round hit. The BRDM (AT-2) has never been exported outside the Soviet Union. This photograph shows a pair of BRDM (AT-2) being preceded by an older BRDM (2P27); all have their weapon bays open and their launchers erected. The circular ports to the right of the rear tactical numbers are the exit ports for the water propulsion system. (Sovfoto)

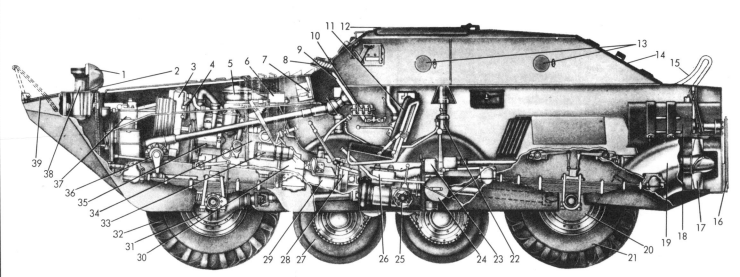

Cross-section of BRDM Scout Car

1. Running light and filter	10. Tyre pressure valve	20. Differential	30. Clutch
2. Night running light	11. Driver's seat	21. Tyre	31. Differential
3. Radiator	12. Main hatch	22. Control for auxiliary wheels	32. Tyre
4. Oil cooler	13. Firing ports	23. Bilge pump	33. Starter
5. Air filter	14. Rear exit	24. Steering control in water	34. Engine
6. Main hydraulic cylinder for brakes	15. Attachment hook	25. Transmission for auxiliary wheels	35. Generator
7. Instrument panel	16. Water jet port	26. Gearbox	36. Steering link
8. Observation port	17. Water jet propeller	27. Auxiliary wheel	37. Air pressure pump for tyres
9. Steering wheel	18. Right fuel tank	28. Brake	38. Capstan
	19. Water jet chamber	29. Transmission	39. Splash plate

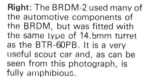

Schmel (Bumblebee). The 2P26 launcher for this weapon was originally mounted on the UAZ-69 jeep. Four launch racks pointed rearward and the gunner sat backwards towards the rear of the vehicle to guide the rocket on its course. The 2P26 could launch four 3M6, but there were no reload rounds. The UAZ-69-2P26 mount was unarmoured, and was nicknamed 'the baby carriage'.

The BRDM had obvious potential as a 3M6 launch vehicle. The rear was modified to accept a simple 3-round 2P27 launcher on an elevating firing rig. Armoured roof panels enclosed the entire array when it was folded down, and the roof panels could be folded over the side of the vehicle when the launch array was elevated. Three spare rounds were stowed internally.

The 3M6 weighs about 55lbs (25kg) and has a fuselage diameter of $5\frac{3}{8}$in (135mm). It has an effective range of 2,750yds (2,500m) and a speed of about 292ft/sec (89m/s). Its shaped charge can penetrate 15in (381mm) of conventional steel armour. The gunner has to keep his eye on both the missile and target and guide the 3M6 by use of a small joystick control while observing the projectile's flight path through a pair of binocular sights. The BRDM (2P27) is being replaced by BRDMs and BRDM-2s fitted with the more effective 9M14M Malyutka.

One of the unique tactical advantages of this type of launch vehicle is that it can be left behind cover while the missile gunner operates his sights from outside the vehicle by using a wire spool. If the gunner is spotted, this tiny sight provides a far smaller target.

The BRDM (2P27) was soon followed by a similar vehicle firing the AT-2 Swatter radio-guided anti-tank missile. The arrangement and characteristics of the launch vehicle were much the same, though the two vehicles are easily distinguishable by different launch racks and a somewhat different folding panel arrangement at the rear. The AT-2A Swatter warhead is capable of penetrating 34in (480mm) of conventional steel armour and has an effective range up to

about 2,750yds (2,500m). The main disadvantage of Swatter is its susceptibility to radio jamming. Its warhead is not armed until 547yds (500m) from the launch vehicle and the original AT-2A missiles are not very responsive to fine control when tracking a moving target.

In the late 1960s, both types began to be replaced by a superior wire guided missile, the 9M14M Malyutka (Sagger AT-3). The Sagger is far smaller than the older 3M6—55lbs (25kg) as opposed to 24½lbs (11.2kg)—has superior armour penetration—15in (381mm) as opposed to nearly 17in (430mm)—and it has better range, 3,250yds (3,000m). Six of these can be carried on the launcher at one time, as opposed to three of the old 3M6. The new BRDM launch vehicle incorporated a simple roof modification that saved time in deploying the launcher rails. Instead of first having to fold down the roof panels over the side, on the newer model the whole roof elevated along with the launch array. As on the earlier models, the launch array had a traverse of about 45° and the fire controls could be moved between 16yds and 109yds (15 to 100m) from the launch vehicle. This vehicle is currently being replaced by the same type of launch rig, but on a more modern BRDM-2 chassis.

The BRDM-2

The BRDM proved a worthwhile scout vehicle, but the rear location of the crew compartment made it difficult to fit it with a small machine-gun turret. As a result, a modernized version was introduced in 1966, the BRDM-2, which had its crew compartment forward and the new engine to the rear. This allowed the designers to fit a 14.5mm KPVT heavy machine-gun turret over the crew section, similar to the turret fitted to the BTR-60PB and the SKOT-2A. The internal space in the BRDM-2 is considerably larger, which has allowed a greater variety of armament and stowage developments.

Three major derivatives of the BRDM-2 followed in short order: the BRDM-2U, which is a command variant with the

BRDM-2 scout car

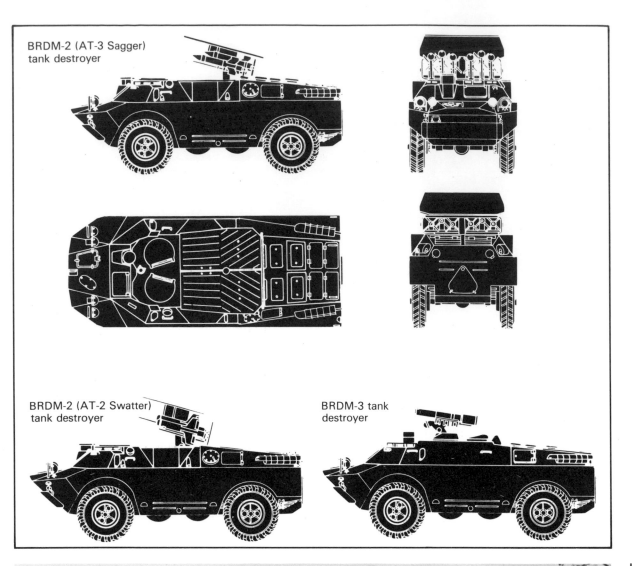

BRDM-2 (AT-3 Sagger)
tank destroyer

BRDM-2 (AT-2 Swatter)
tank destroyer

BRDM-3 tank
destroyer

Left: The BRDM-2 (9M14M Malyutka) tank destroyer does away with the turret of the standard BRDM-2 in favour of a six-missile launcher array under an armoured roof. When not in use, the whole array folds neatly into the hull cavity, where a further 14 rounds can be stored. The optical sight for the missiles is housed in the small container on the vehicle's front starboard quarter. Many of these vehicles are being retrofitted with semi-automatic guidance, so that they may be fitted with the new modified Sagger. (Sovfoto)

Right: The BRDM-3 is armed with the new AT-5 guided anti-tank missile, which is very similar to the Milan in service with NATO. It has five launch tubes on a traversable platform, a tracking sight to the right behind the assistant driver's position and a reload hatch behind the missile array. It has the modified rear engine deck seen since the introduction of the BRDM-2 (9M14M). The related infantry version of the AT-5 has been given the NATO designation of AT-4. (US Army)

turret removed, and a power generator put in its place on the hull roof to power the extra radio transmitters; BRDM-2rkh, which is comparable to the earlier BRDM-rkh and has marking flag dispensers at the hull rear to designate chemically or radioactively contaminated zones; and a tank destroyer version similar to the BRDM (9M14M) was also put in service. A six-rail launcher is mounted in mid-section, with an additional fourteen rounds stowed internally. The gunner sits to the right of the driver and has an elevating periscopic control sight in front of him. As on the earlier BRDM tank destroyers, the rockets can be fired remotely from a portable joystick control pack.

In 1974, a new mobile anti-aircraft version was unveiled in Warsaw, the BRDM-2 (SA-9 Gaskin). The first model, called the BRDM-2(A)(1) by the US Army, has two dielectric boxes on the front of the hull and one centred over the engine deck, and a square box on the left side of the turret. The more commonly seen BRDM-2(A)(2) has none of these containers. The SA-9 is a low-altitude infrared heat seeking missile fired from a four-tube launcher on top of the vehicle. The entire launch array folds down for travel.

In the November 1977 parade in Moscow, the first of a new generation of Soviet tank destroyers based on the BRDM-2 was unveiled. The new launch system, given the US designation AT-5, is a wire guided second generation anti-tank missile launcher very similar to the Franco-German Milan. The entire arrangement has been tentatively identified as the BRDM-3. Each vehicle carries five launch tubes. The BRDM-3 has an optical sight and IR goniometer for missile tracking similar to that on the BRDM-2 (AT-2b). In contrast to the earlier anti-tank missiles, the AT-5 does not require the gunner to keep track of both missiles and target. The semi-active IR homing allows the gunner to concentrate solely on the target, with the fire controls correcting the missile's path accordingly. While Western analysts are very sceptical of Sagger's performance, except when used en masse or in the hands of an exceptionally well-trained user, the semi-automatic system of the AT-5 is an entirely different matter.

The AT-5 probably flies at about 165-220yds/sec (150-200m/sec) and can probably penetrate 19½in-23½in (500-600mm) of conventional steel armour. The more

sophisticated fire controls of the BRDM-3 make it extremely unlikely that they can be moved away from the vehicle as on previous types.

With the advent of the AT-5, and a ground launched relative, the Fagot (Basoon, known in the US as the AT-4), there has been a surge of modification work on existing tank destroyers. There are reports that a new version of the 9M14M is also fitted with semi-automatic IR guidance. In 1977, photographs were first published of a new version of the BRDM-2 fitted with a quadruple Swatter launcher similar to that used with the Sagger. It is extremely unlikely that an outdated radio-controlled rocket such as this would be given a new launch vehicle unless its fire controls had been modified. This has led to speculation that it too has been fitted with a new guidance system with semi-active IR/radio terminal homing. It is expected that this new Swatter, AT-2b, has an increased range of about 3,850yds (3,500m). The Swatter AT-2b is also used on the Mi-24 Hind-D assault helicopter.

The new semi-automatic fire control systems now being introduced into service have brought the Soviet Ground Forces much closer to the technologically more sophisticated systems used by NATO, and there is every reason to believe that either they have or will have a new missile, using semi-active laser illumination guidance, comparable to the American Hellfire laser beam rider. This will probably first appear on the Hind Mi-24 assault helicopter and eventually on a BRDM tank destroyer.

In spite of the growing sophistication of these weapons, all depend on a shaped charge warhead. None is large enough to carry an effective HEAT round and they are all too slow to employ a kinetic penetrator. If reports are correct, the new Chobham armour is virtually invulnerable to shaped charge weapons. Non Chobham-armoured vehicles will be in abundance for a decade, but as more composite armoured tanks enter service, the utility of such missile-armed tank destroyers will drop accordingly.

The FUG

In the late 1960s, the Hungarians began their own programme to replace the older BRDM, and produced the D-442 FUG (Felderito Uszo Gepkocsi). This appeared in service in 1964 and was widely adopted by Warsaw Pact forces outside the Soviet Union. The initial version was a

FUG scout transporter

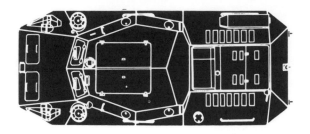

SOVIET ANTI-TANK GUIDED MISSILES

Soviet designation:	3M6 Schmel	—	—	9M14M Malyutka	Fagot	—
US system designation:	AT-1	AT-2a	AT-2b	AT-3	AT-4	AT-5
NATO missile designation:	Snapper	Swatter	Swatter (Mod 1)	Sagger	—	—
Guidance:	Wire guided, opt. track	Radio	Radio with terminal homing	Wire guided, opt. track	Semi-automatic	Semi-automatic
Probability of a hit:	90 per cent	88 per cent	80-90 per cent	88 per cent	—	—
Probability of a kill:	67 per cent	67 per cent	67 per cent	69 per cent	—	—
Remote control:	Up to 55yds (50m)	—	—	16-110yds (15-100m)	—	—
Cruising speed:	291ft/sec (88.8m/sec)	—	492ft/sec (150m/sec)	393ft/sec (120m/sec)	492—657ft/sec (150-200m/sec)	—
Maximum flight time:	28 sec	—	23 sec	27 sec	13 sec	—
Minimum range:	164yds (150m)	550yds (500m)	550yds (500m)	550-875yds (500-800m)	—	—
Maximum range:	2,736yds (2,500m)	2,736yds (2,500m)	3,830yds (3,500m)	3,283yds (3,000m)	2,189yds (2,000m)	4,378yds (4,000m)
Missile length:	3.5ft (1.1m)	—	4ft (1.2m)	2.3ft (.86m)	—	4ft (1.2m)
Fuselage diameter:	5.25in (135mm)	—	5.125in (132mm)	4.75in (119mm)	—	5.25in (133mm)
Wing diameter:	2.45ft (740mm)	2.15ft (660mm)	2.15ft (660mm)	1.5ft (460mm)	—	—
Launch weight:	54lbs (24.31kg)	59lbs (26.76kg)	65lbs (29.48kg)	25lbs (11.29kg)	11lbs (5.0kg)	—
Warhead type:	HEAT	HEAT	HEAT	HEAT	HEAT	HEAT
Warhead weight:	12lbs (5.28kg)	—	—	6lbs (2.72kg)	—	—
Penetration performance:	15in (380mm)	19in (480mm)	19.75in (500mm)	17in (430mm)	19.75-24in (500-600mm)	—
Launcher type:	Rail	Rail	Rail	Rail	Rail(?)	Tube
Launch vehicle:	UAZ-69 (2P26) BRDM (2P27)	BRDM BRDM-2	BRDM BRDM-2	Manpack BRDM BRDM-2 BMP-1 BMD-1	Manpack	BRDM-3
Helicopter launcher:	MI-2 MI-4 MI-8	MI-24	MI-24	MI-2 MI-8 MI-24		

turretless transporter similar to the BTR-60P but, in 1966, a version with a small cast turret was seen at a parade in Budapest, and called the FUG-66. It was in fact the pre-production prototype of the D-944, PSzH-Iv, which entered service in 1970. The PSzH-IV was also called the FUG-70 or FUG-2, and was fitted with a new welded-plate turret. The Czech Army adopted large numbers of these instead of the BRDM-2, designating them OT-65 for the FUG and OT-66 for the PSzH-IV. A special version, mounting the same small turret with 81mm recoilless T-21 gun as the OT-62, was also built for Czech service, as well as an ambulance version.

As in the case of the BRDM and BRDM-2, there is a special NBC troop vehicle with marking flag dispensers, as well as another chemical decontamination vehicle, which carries a small tent to be fitted to the rear for hosing down contaminated troops and equipment. Unlike the BRDM family, the FUG series have not yet been modified into tank destroyers. A turretless command vehicle based on the PSz H-IV exists.

RECONNAISSANCE VEHICLES

	BRDM	BRDM-2	FUG	PSzH-IV
Weight:	5.6 tonnes	7.0 tonnes	6.1 tonnes	7.0 tonnes
Crew:	4-5	4	5	3+6
Length:	18.75ft (5.7m)	18.875ft (5.75m)	19ft (5.79m)	19ft (5.79m)
Width:	7ft (2.2m)	7.5ft (2.3m)	8ft (2.5m)	8ft (2.5m)
Height:	6ft (1.9m)	7.5ft (2.3m)	6ft (1.9m)	8ft (2.5m)
Ground clearance:	12.375in (315mm)	13.125in (335mm)	13.375in (340mm)	13.375in (340mm)
Engine:	GAZ-4OP	GAZ-41	Csepel D-414.44	Raba-MAN D-2156
Horsepower:	90	140	100	120
Range:	310 miles (500km)	465 miles (750mm)	310 miles (500km)	310 miles (500km)
Maximum speed:	50mph (80km/hr)	62mph (100km/hr)	50mph (80km/hr)	62mph (100km/hr)
Swimming speed:	5mph (9km/hr)	6mph (10km/hr)	5-6mph (8-10km/hr)	6mph (10km/hr)
Main Armament:	SGMB 7.62mm	KPVT 14.5mm	SGMB 7.62mm	KPVT 14.5mm
Rounds stowed:	1,250	500	1,250	500
Armour:	.375in (10mm)	.375in (10mm)	.375in (10mm)	.375in (10mm)

Left: The Hungarian FUG (Felderito Uszo Gepkosci) can be used either as a scout car in place of the BRDM-2, or as a small troop transporter. Here, the vehicle is being used in the latter rôle by a Bulgarian infantry squad. The trooper in the foreground is armed with an RPG-7 grenade launcher. (Bulgarian Embassy via George Balin)

Left: The Czechoslovak Army is one of the largest users of the FUG and its derivatives. These two vehicles are decontamination scout cars. They have the same type of marking system on the rear as that used on the Soviet BRDM-rkh. The Czechoslovak versions of the standard FUG are designated OT-65.

Centre: The Czechoslovak Army has developed a version of the OT-65 with the same type of small sub-turret used on the OT-62, armed with the 82mm Tarašnice recoilless rifle. This vehicle is using the autumn camouflage pattern without the bright ochre stripes.

Bottom: A heavily modified version of the FUG, designated the PSzH-IV, was designed by the Hungarians as a counterpart to the BRDM-2. The vehicle shown here is in Czechoslovak service, and is designated OT-66. (Eastfoto)

Mechanized Artillery

Soviet wartime self-propelled gun development centred principally around heavily armoured assault guns such as the medium SU-85, SU-100, and the heavy ISU-122, ISU-122s and ISU-152. These weapons were all excellent tank destroyers that could also be used to provide direct high-explosive fire support for infantry or armoured units. Soviet development of tracked field artillery comparable to the American 'Priest', British/Canadian 'Sexton' or German 'Hummel', which was used primarily for indirect fire support, was far less pronounced. Only the light SU-76 fits into this category, and it should be kept in mind that even this vehicle was originally designed as a tank destroyer. Output of these vehicles was prodigious; SU-76 production alone was half as large as the total of all German tanks and self-propelled guns manufactured during the war.

After the war, the light SU-76 was gradually withdrawn from service, though it did see extensive action in the Korean War. The SU-100 lingered on until the introduction in 1947 of an improved model that incorporated progressive developments in sighting equipment, increased ammunition stowage, and an uprated engine. With the advent of the T-54, it was eventually phased out. The only wartime type to see prolonged service in the Cold War years was the ISU-152. Many were re-manufactured as the improved ISU-152K with the newer V-54-K engine, improved sighting, added external stowage and other new features. Production ceased in 1947. These remained in service until the early 1960s and, by now, most have been converted to recovery tractors and repair vehicles.

Most of the Soviets' projects during the Cold War focussed on the tank destroyer variety of self-propelled guns. Their first attempt was to try to mate a T-34 chassis with a 122mm gun. It was similar to an experiment on a modified SU-122 chassis in 1943, and the scheme proved

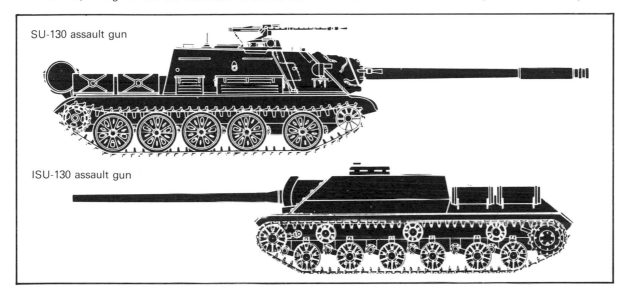

SU-130 assault gun

ISU-130 assault gun

Left: Since the war, the Soviet Union has plunged ahead with the development of conventional tank destroyers. Here is an example based on a T-55 chassis. These vehicles are rarely seen, and may be designated SU-130. The provisioning of a stereoscopic rangefinder over the gunner's position is a good indication that the vehicle was intended for long-range fire support.

unworkable due to the small size of the chassis. An improved version of the ISU-122, possibly designated ISU-130, using a 130mm gun on an IS-3 chassis only got as far as the prototype stage. In the 1950s a variety of experiments were conducted using various types of guns on a T-54 and T-55 chassis. A casemated, fully enclosed tank destroyer with limited gun traverse, and probably using the M-46 130mm divisional gun, entered production in small numbers. It may have been designated SU-130, but there is very little information available. It was one of the few Soviet vehicles of the time fitted with a stereoscopic rangefinder, and was intended for long-range tank duels. It entered service with the Soviet Ground Forces in European Russia in the 1960s, and a similarly enigmatic model based on the T-62 replaced it in the early 1970s but apparently in only small numbers on a trial basis. It does not appear that either type was appreciated, as both have turned up recently, with their guns removed, in use as armoured recovery vehicles.

It is not entirely surprising that these tank destroyer types have not seen widespread use. Tank destroyers such as the SU-85 and SU-100 were introduced for two reasons: the contemporary medium tank, the T-34, was inadequate against the heavier German tanks (for example, the Royal Tiger); and, secondly, a tank destroyer was cheaper to build than a comparably-armed heavy tank. However, since the 1950s, medium tanks such as the T-54 and T-55 have been armed with a very effective gun that can defeat nearly any existing NATO tank type. Therefore, supplementary types such as the heavy tank and the tank destroyer are redundant. The only case where tank destroyers still play a role is with airborne units, where their weight advantage makes them necessary.

While the demise of the tank destroyer was not unexpected, the lapse in Soviet interest in self-propelled field-guns was quite startling. With the advent of sophisticated fire-location radars, conventional towed field artillery became extremely vulnerable to counter-battery fire. For many NATO units, the time consuming process of emplacing and moving field-guns, even with prime movers and gun tractors, has largely been removed by using self-propelled mounts. Assault guns like the ISU-152K are not really suitable due to their limited stowage capacity and limited elevation. Moreover, most modern self-propelled guns have their armament in fully traversable turrets or at least on fully traversable open platforms.

In the late 1960s, the Soviet Union finally began developing weapons of this type. They were issued to the troops in the early 1970s. The first type, mounting a 122mm gun-howitzer, was seen at the 22 July parade in Warsaw in 1974, and a second type, mounting a 152mm gun, began appearing in Soviet press photographs during the following year. Both types were displayed at the 7 November 1977 parade in Moscow. The designations for these vehicles have not yet been declassified, and Western sources have been referring to them as the Self-propelled Howitzer 122mm M-1974 and the Self-propelled Gun-howitzer 152mm M-1973, or SAU-122 and SAU-152 for the sake of convenience in this discussion, though it should be kept in mind that these are not their proper Soviet designations.

Left: A vehicle similar to the SU-130 was built on the T-62 chassis. Though the actual tank destroyer version has never been seen, a modified armoured recovery vehicle based on it, the T-62-T, was photographed at a recent Moscow parade. (US Army)

Left: The first of the new Soviet self-propelled guns to be publicly displayed was this 122mm howitzer type. In lieu of its correct Soviet designation, which is still classified, it has been called the SAU-122 or M-1974 122mm self-propelled gun.

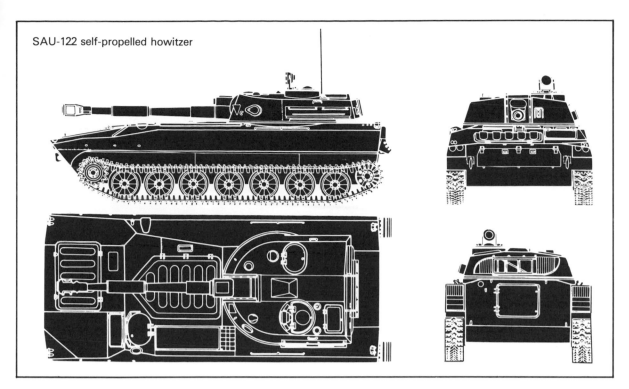

SAU-122 self-propelled howitzer

Left: This side view of an SAU-122 shows how long and sleek it is. The vehicle is fully amphibious, and has passive starlight scopes for night driving.

The SAU-122

Both designs are fairly conventional and resemble comparable NATO types. The SAU-122 is a 22-tonne fully amphibious vehicle with a 122mm howitzer, which is probably a derivative of the 122mm D-30 howitzer, in a fully enclosed, fully traversable turret. The gun has a maximum elevation of about 40°. It has an effective range of 9-15 miles (15-24km) and a maximum rate of fire of about 8 rounds per minute, although its sustained rate of fire is probably closer to three rounds per minute. The vehicle has a four-man crew, and is fitted with an NBC filtration system.

Automotively, the SAU-122 is a derivative of the new MT-L family of tractors using the YaMZ-238 high-compression 240hp V-8 engine. The main advantage of this new family over the older PT-76 derived types, stems not only from the more powerful engine, but from the fact that the YaMZ-238 is a common power plant in a wide range of civilian and military heavy truck types, which will lead to simplified supplies. The SAU-122 can be fitted with two different types of Hadfield steel tracks: a conventional type, and a wider track with grousers for operation on soft ground.

Though the commander has been provided with a standard OU-3GK infra-red searchlight and corresponding viewing periscopes, it seems likely that PNV-37 or PNV 57 night vision devices have been fitted. Fire control is provided by the new BMP-SON radar direction vehicle and the new M-1976 artillery command/reconnaissance vehicle. It is believed that the new SAU-122 batteries consist of six SAU 122s supported by a single BMP-SON and M-1976 artillery command vehicle.

The SAU-152

The SAU-152 is quite similar in general layout to the SAU-122, but it is not amphibious. Its gun is derived from the D-20 152mm Model 1955 gun-howitzer and has an effective range of about 10 miles (17km). With rocket-assisted rounds, this range can be boosted to 18 miles (30km). The gun is fully traversable and can be elevated from −3° to 65°. The chassis is automotively derived from the SA-4 Ganef missile transporter and is fitted with a 500hp diesel engine. The SAU-152 has a maximum rate of fire of about four rounds per minute and a sustained rate of about two rounds per minute. It is believed to have a five-man crew and weigh about 25 to 30 tonnes. In common

Above: A battery of SAU-122 come under mock attack during training in the winter of 1978. The main gun can be elevated to 45° for firing. (Sovfoto)

Left: The SAU-122 was first seen at the Liberation Day parade in Warsaw in 1974. Subsequently, it has turned up in Soviet and Czechoslovak service as well. This Polish battery is being prepared to move out.

Right, top: A BMP-1 infantry combat vehicle. (US Army)

Right, bottom: An ASU-57 assault gun. (US Army)

Left, top and bottom: Two views of an ASU-85 tank destroyer; note the ISU-122 self-propelled howitzer in the bottom photograph.

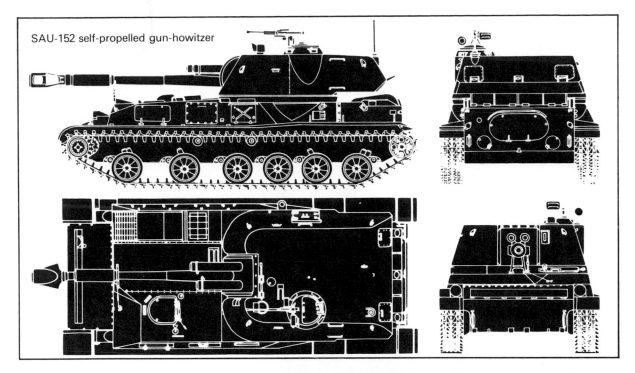

SAU-152 self-propelled gun-howitzer

Right: The enormous turret on the SAU-152 has led some to suspect that an automatic loader may be fitted, but this is conjecture at the moment. The SAU-152 is too heavy to be amphibious, and does not appear to have provisions for a snorkel; therefore, it must be floated across rivers on a GSP ferry (Gusenichnii Samokhodnii Parom or tracked ferry vehicle). (US Army)

Right: The wheel spacing on the SAU-152 has been arranged to best distribute the heavy weight of the main gun at the rear of the chassis. (US Army)

Left: An overhead shot of the SAU-152 (Soviet designation unknown). The chassis on which it is built has been derived from the SA-4 Ganef transporter, and is also used on the new GMZ minelayer. (US Army)

Left: This rear view of the SAU-152 (also known as the 152mm self-propelled gun M1973) shows the large rear hatch used for replenishing the ammunition supply. (US Army)

Left: To support the new self-propelled guns, a special support vehicle was developed on the chassis of the new MT-L tractor. Three versions of this armoured command vehicle have been identified, all with varying optical and electronic equipment. This photograph shows the first model. Judging from its large size, it is probably also used to carry extra ammunition for the guns. (Sovfoto)

SELF-PROPELLED GUNS

	ISU-152K	SU-130*	SAU-122*	SAU-152*
Weight:	47.2 tonnes	40 tonnes	23 tonnes	28 tonnes
Crew:	5	4	4	5
Length, overall:	29ft (8.9m)	—	24ft (7.3m)	26ft (7.8m)
Length of hull:	22ft (6.7m)	21ft (6.4m)	24ft (7.3m)	23ft (7.1m)
Width:	10.5ft (3.2m)	11ft (3.3m)	10ft (3.0m)	10.5ft (3.2m)
Height:	8ft (2.4m)	8ft (2.4m)	8ft (2.4m)	9ft (2.7m)
Ground clearance:	17.5in (440mm)	16.5in (420mm)	18in (460mm)	17.625in (450mm)
Maximum speed:	25mph (40km/hr)	31mph (50km/hr)	28mph (45km/hr)	31mph (50km/hr)
Engine:	V-54K	V-55	YaMZ-238	—
Horsepower:	520	580	240	500
Armament:	152mm ML-20S	130mm M-46S	122mm D-30S	152mm D-20S
Length of barrel in calibres:	33.5	55	35	29
Maximum range:	7 miles (12.2km)	5 miles (8.0km)	9.5 miles (15.3km)	11.5 miles (18.4km)
Maximum rate of fire:	3rpm	6rpm	8rpm	4rpm
Sustained rate of fire:	2rpm	4rpm	3rpm	2rpm
Projectile weight (HE round):	86-95lbs (39-43kg)	73lbs (33kg)	49lbs (22kg)	97lbs (44kg)
Elevation:	−3° to +20°	−2° to 120°	−5° to +40°	−3° to +65°
Traverse:	10°	10°	360°	360°

*provisional data

with the SAU-122, it is supported by a BMP-SON and M-1976 artillery command vehicle.

The SAU-122 and SAU-152 compare very favourably with their nearest NATO counterparts, the Abbot and the M 109 A1. The SAU-122 is particularly attractive due to its excellent amphibious characteristics. Soviet Ground Forces still lack a heavy long-range mobile artillery piece comparable to the American M-107 175mm long-range gun, but some recent Soviet publications have shown what appears to be a model of a 203mm self-propelled gun. So far, the SAU-152 is limited to service with the Soviet Ground Forces, but the SAU-122 is in use with the Polish,

Czechoslovak and East German armies. It is likely that SAU-122 production has already begun in either Poland or Czechoslovakia, or both.

The new M-1976 artillery command vehicle is an automotive relative of the MT-L/SAU-122 family and is fully amphibious. At least three versions are now in service. The earliest type is fitted with a DShK 12.7mm machine-gun, while subsequent models do not have this anti-aircraft weapon but have additional optical and radio equipment. It is possible that variants of this vehicle carry supplementary ammunition for the SAU-122 and SAU-152.

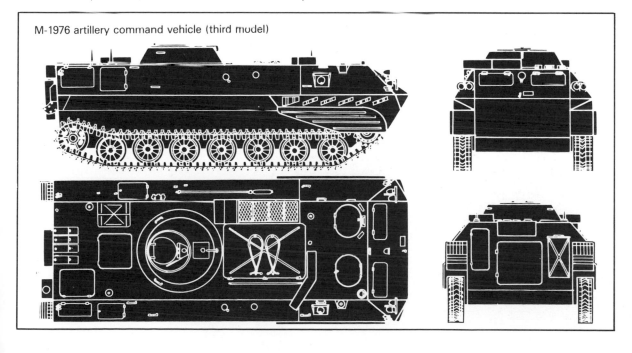

M-1976 artillery command vehicle (third model)

Mechanized Air Defence

One of the most apparent gaps in the arsenal of the Red Army for most of the Second World War was their lack of any mobile anti-aircraft vehicles. The ZSU-37, which entered production at the end of the war, was not entirely satisfactory due to various problems, including slow turret traverse, so other more fruitful approaches were tried.

Work progressed along two avenues: a simple, light, wheeled mount for the KPV heavy 14.5mm machine-gun, and a tracked mount for the new 57mm Model 1950 S-60 anti-aircraft gun. A twin-barrelled version of the KPV, the ZPU-2, was chosen and mounted on a largely unmodified BTR-152 and BTR-40 chassis. These were referred to as BTR-ZPU. They were widely used in the 1950s and early 1960s, particularly in the air defence companies of the motorized rifle regiments. Polish marine units (Jednostki Obrony Wybrzeża or JOW) also used a similar arrangement, which was fitted to the K-61 amphibious transporter for beachhead defence during amphibious operations. The Czech Army developed independently its own weapon, an M53/59 twin-barrelled 30mm autocannon mounted on an armoured Praga V3S truck and based around the 30mm PL dvojkanonu vz.53 ZK453 gun system. The Czechs usually

Left: A BTR-152 in service with the East German Army. This vehicle offered rather more room for the ZPU-2 mount, and was the more common of the BTR-ZPU types.

Left: These Polish JOW units (Jednostki Obrony Wybrzeża or Coastal Defence Units) are using a ZPU-2 mounted in a spacious K-61 hold for beachhead defence during an amphibious operation.

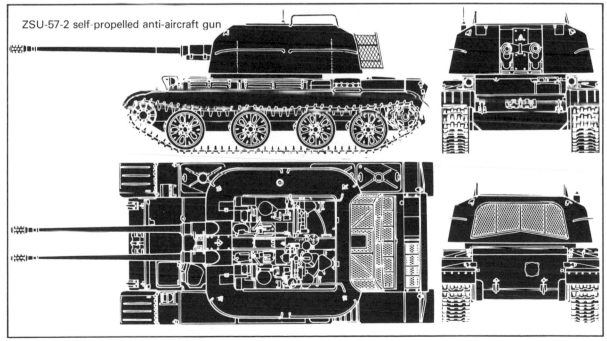

ZSU-57-2 self-propelled anti-aircraft gun

refer to this vehicle as the PLdvK 30mm. An updated version, permitting the gun to be ground emplaced, is designated Mk 53/70.

The KPV vehicles are reasonably effective against propeller-driven attack aircraft, helicopters and early generation low-flying jets, but their slow traverse speeds, simple fire control, and limited range make them less effective against modern air threats. Their maximum range is roughly 8,755yds (8,000m) horizontal and 5,472yds (5,000m) vertical, and their effective range is about 1,532yds (1,400m). They are no longer in service in large numbers.

The ZSU-57-2

The S-60 development programme led to the appearance in 1952 of a twin-barrelled version, the S-68. It was a very satisfactory design, being heavily influenced by wartime German research. A mobile mount was contemplated, and this version entered service in 1957 as the ZSU-57-2. It was issued to the new air defence regiments of the tank and motorized rifle divisions. The ZSU-57-2 was based on the T-54 chassis, but as its components and armour were lighter than the tank version, it was possible to modify the suspension and reduce the number of main road wheels to four. The S-68 mount was fitted into a very large, boxy,

open-topped turret with very light armour protection. Each gun has a maximum rate of fire of 120 rounds per minute, and 316 rounds are usually stowed. The vehicle is fitted with conventional optical sights, which give it an effective range of 4,375yds (4,000m). Although it cannot be linked to the PUAZO-6/60 director or SON-9 and 9A radars, which are used with the S-60 static mount, it can be used to engage ground targets. There is a very effective APHE round available for it that can penetrate 4in (103mm) of armour at 545yds (500m). As a result, the ZSU-57-2 crews are trained for anti-tank defence in tight circumstances. It should be noted, though, that the ammunition for the ZSU-57-2 is not interchangeable with that for the ZIS-2 or Ch-51 57mm anti-tank guns, as it uses a different casing shape.

When firing, the ZSU-57-2 is usually crewed by six men: a driver, two loaders, two gunners and a gun commander. A large screened basket for catching spent shell casings is fitted aft the turret. There were two production models of the ZSU-57-2: an earlier model using the automotive components of the early T-54, and a later production type using later T-54 components. The later production type can be readily identified by the two small hinged ports, which the earlier model did not have, on the upper front of the turret. These were used for sighting.

Since 1960 the ZSU-57-2 has been standard equipment throughout the Warsaw Pact countries, and has been widely exported. It saw service in the Middle East in 1967 and 1973, and in Vietnam in 1972 and 1973. While in service with the North Vietnamese Army, it was primarily for mobile convoy defence against roving American fighter-bombers, though occasionally it was used against ground targets. It is currently being withdrawn from front line service in the Soviet, Polish and East German armies in favour of the ZSU-23-4 Shilka.

The main tactical limitation of the ZSU-57-2 was its lack of onboard radar. This limited its operations to clear days with good visibility. About one-third of autumn and winter mornings in Central Europe are foggy, and a similar proportion of days during these seasons have ceilings below 2,450ft (750m). Even during optimum summer months, 50 per cent cloud cover below 3,250ft (1,000m) occurs for 15 per cent of the days, thus restricting the employment of optically-sighted weapons such as the S-68 on the ZSU-57-2.

The ZSU-23-4 Shilka

Design of a new system, centred around the four-barrelled ZU-23 autocannon, began in the late 1950s using a chassis related to the PT-76/GT tractor series. Entering service in 1965, the ZSU-23-4 Shilka eliminated the primary technical flaw of the ZSU-57-2 by mounting an onboard all-weather radar at the rear of its gun turret. Shilka proved an immediate success in Soviet service, and at least eight identifiable production models have so far appeared. The earliest cluster of these variations had fairly clean turrets with a minimum of external stowage, and can be distinguished from one another by small details such as heat ducts and air intakes. The intermediate production types all had new, large, ammunition stowage bins fitted to the forward corners of the turret sides. The latest model, sometimes referred to as the ZSU-23-4M, is an improvement on the intermediate types, and is suspected to carry a digital computer in place of the older analogue computer used in earlier versions.

Shilka is centred around the AZP-23 quadruple 23mm autocannon, which has a maximum rate of fire of 3,400 rounds per minute, or about 14 rounds per second from any one barrel. In practice, the guns are usually fired in short bursts, which can be set at either 3-5 rounds per barrel or 5-10 rounds. Against very fast-flying jets, it can be fired in bursts of 50 rounds per barrel. There are two types of ammunition available: an HE-fragmentation round with a $6\frac{2}{3}$ oz (.19kg) projectile for use against aircraft or helicopters, and a special armour-piercing/incendiary round for use against ground targets. Both rounds travel at about 1,062yds/sec (970m/s). The API round weighs $6\frac{2}{3}$ oz (.189kg) and can penetrate 1in (25mm) of armour at 545yds (500m). A standard three-and-a-half second burst unleashes about 84lbs (38kg) of steel and explosives against the target. Both ammunition types have a tracer base, so Shilka gives off quite a fireworks and smoke display when it lets loose. Two thousand rounds of ammunition are stored in four compartments at the front of the turret on link belts, and it is common practice to mix the rounds, with one round of API for every three rounds of HE-Frag.

The maximum range of the AZP-23 is 7,500yds (7,000m) horizontally and 5,500yds (5,100m) vertically, though the effective range is closer to 2,750yds (2,500m) with optical sights and 3,250yds (3,000m) with the radar. In 1973, Israeli

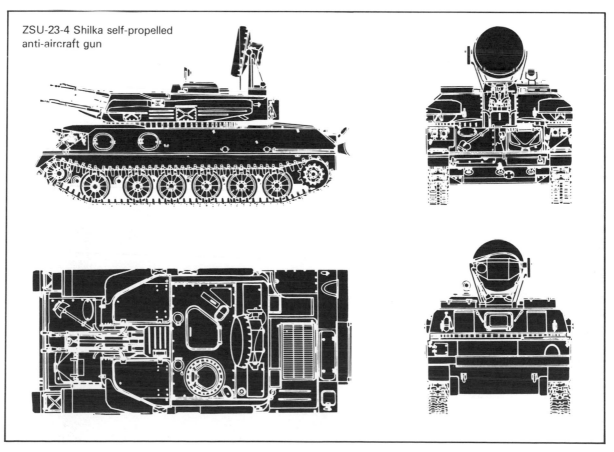

ZSU-23-4 Shilka self-propelled anti-aircraft gun

pilots learnt from experience that to remain in the sights of a Shilka at 2,150-2,750yds (2,000-2,500m) for 35 seconds is lethal, and shorter exposures at closer ranges provide the same unwelcome result. A single round from the 23mm gun can cripple most modern aircraft if it strikes a vital area, and a single round into the rotor of most current helicopters will shatter it and lead to the loss of the craft.

The gun is crewed by a radar search operator, a range operator and a commander, who are all located in the turret, and the fourth crew member, the driver, sits in the hull on the left. The gun itself is located behind bulkheads to prevent the leakage of propellant gases into the crew compartment. It can be fired manually or under automatic radar direction. Generally, it is manually operated when firing against ground targets, or when a systems failure in the radar, computer or gun stabilizer forces its use. The gun control system consists of four basic components: the Gun Dish radar, the optical sights, the analogue computer (or, possibly, in the case of the ZSU-23-4M, a digital ballistic computer) and a two-plane stabilization system.

The Gun Dish radar operates in the 14.6 to 15.6 GHz range. A large parabolic reflector antenna is mounted on the rear of the turret, covered with a radio wave-passing screen and fitted with a horn-type exciter. The radar searches, identifies the target, automatically tracks it and provides both target range and angular position. Should the target move from the scanning area, servo drives automatically adjust the antenna to reacquire the target.

When visibility is good, the optical fire sights can be linked with the angular position-guide of the radar. The computer is used mainly to provide adequate lead angles when engaging fast-moving aircraft, and it receives input regarding target coordinates and speed either from the radar or the optical gun sights. Western analysts who have examined the analogue computer feel it is relatively outdated, though certainly very functional, and there is speculation that newer models have a digital computer.

The stabilization system is linked to an azimuth gyro that keeps the radar antenna and gun sights on target in spite of the pitch and roll of the vehicle over rough terrain. Automatically, through servo systems, it alters the antenna and gun sight angle accordingly. A kinematic roll circuit is built into the whole stabilizing network to alter the antenna direction in the horizontal plane when the turret is traversed.

The search operator and range operator locate a target while the radar is in its surveillance or sector-scan mode.

Once discovered, the radar is switched to an automatic tracking mode. The target is then identified as friend or foe as the coordinate data are fed into the computer to obtain proper gun lead. As soon as the computer has the lead, the AZP-23 is automatically brought to bear on the target and is fed a continuous stream of corrections. When these corrections have been completed, the radar operator or commander signals the crew by saying "we have data", and the gun opens fire.

The optical sight uses a conventional set of gun aspect rings to determine lead angle, but this is only used for airborne targets when one of the major gun control systems has suffered a failure.

Shilka is powered by a modified PT-76 engine, the V-6R, but due to the power needs of the turret and all of the electronic equipment, a subsidiary DG4M-1 gas turbine power generator is also fitted. As in most tanks, the driver and commander are both provided with gyroscopically linked navigation equipment to help plot the course and location. Shilka is also fitted with an NBC filtration system, cabin overpressure and radiation and chemical sensors to prevent air contaminants from causing crew casualties. A pair of FG-125 infra-red lights are located on either side of the driver. The commander is provided with a TKN-1T night periscopic infra-red scanner with an effective viewing range of 220-275yds (200-250m), and the driver has a TVN-2 infra-red periscope which, with the FG-125 illuminated, provides about a 45yd (40m) viewing range at night.

The ZSU-23-4 has proved to be an extremely effective system, particularly when used in conjunction with the newer Soviet surface-to-air missiles. It poses a very serious threat to most assault helicopters and to those unlucky attack aircraft that stray within its lethal radius without adequate ECM protection to jam its radar. While new ECM techniques have been developed on the basis of captured Shilkas, it is likely that progressive improvements in the Gun Dish system will lessen the effect of these attempts and prompt another cycle of countermeasures.

In the 1973 Arab-Israeli war, Shilka proved especially deadly when paired with the SA-6 Gainful missile. Israeli pilots were unable to jam Gainful's radar and tried various evasion techniques, often running into accompanying batteries of Shilkas, with dire results. Some press reports indicate that of the one hundred aircraft losses suffered by the Israeli Air Force, about fifty were accountable to this cause.

Left: The intermediate family of ZSU-23-4 variants had new large stowage bins fitted to the turret's front quarter. This dramatically increased the ammunition stowage. These two ZSU-23-4 are protecting a platoon of T-54Bs as they traverse an old, dried out river bed. The two bucket-shaped covers over the optical sights have been folded open for possible use; the gun commander scans the sky visually as does the radar electronically. (Sovfoto)

Bottom, left: From the right side, the new ZSU-23-4M can barely be distinguished from the earlier models, except for a new access port behind the two forward ones on the side of the hull. The new rain cover over the AZP-23 gun mount also provides a clue. (US Army)

Bottom, centre: A view of the starboard side of the new ZSU-23-4M. This photograph clearly shows the vehicle's many new fittings, which have led some Western analysts to suggest it is fitted with a new digital targeting computer. The pentagonal protrusion above the Guards Division marking and the rounded cover above it are the primary identifying features of this model. (US Army)

Bottom, right: This overhead view shows the long bulbous external pannier on the turret sides of an intermediate production ZSU-23-4. (US Army)

SELF-PROPELLED ANTI-AIRCRAFT GUNS

	ZSU-57-2	ZSU-23-4
Weight:	28.1 tonnes	14 tonnes
Crew:	6	4
Length:	27ft (8.4m)	21ft (6.3m)
Width:	10ft (3.2m)	9ft (2.9m)
Height:	9ft (2.7m)	7ft* (2.2m)
Engine:	V-54 diesel	V-6R diesel
Horsepower:	520	240
Fuel capacity:	179 gallons (812 litres)	52 gallons (250 litres)
Range:	248 miles (400km)	161 miles (260km)
Maximum speed:	30mph (48km/hr)	27mph (44km/hr)
Armour:	.625in (15mm)	.625in (15mm)
Main gun:	57mm S-68	23mm AZP-23
Elevation:	−5 to 85°	−7 to 80°
Rounds stowed:	316	2,000
Fire control:	optical	radar/optical

*radar folded down in travelling position

Left: The SA-2 Guideline is one of the oldest missile weapons used by the PVO-SV (Ground Forces Air Defence). These two V750K missiles on their loading trailers are being towed by the new ATS-59-V tractor. (Sovfoto)

Right: The SA-4 Ganef was the first fully mobile anti-aircraft missile used by PVO-SV. This particular Ganef battery uses the newer model with the improved launch vehicle. (Sovfoto)

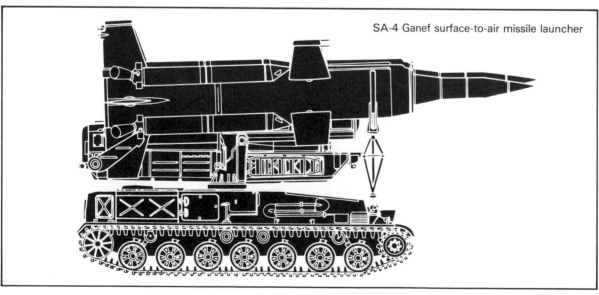

SA-4 Ganef surface-to-air missile launcher

There are fairly obvious limitations in mobile gun-based anti aircraft systems and, over the past decade, this has led to the development of a family of mobile anti-aircraft missiles.

In the mid-1960s, the Air Defence Regiments received their first V75SM (SA-2 Guideline) and SA-3 batteries. The SA-2 had already been in service with the PVO-Strany (Homeland Air Defence), for the protection of static defence positions and military installations in the Soviet Union, and was responsible for the downing of Francis Gary Powers' U-2 high-altitude reconnaissance aeroplane on 1 May 1960.

The SA-2 is a two-stage air defence weapon, with a liquid booster and a liquid fuel sustainer. It uses a radio/homing guidance system in conjunction with the Fan Song radar operating in the 2.94-3.06 GHz frequency band. The modified V750VK has a vertical range of 15 miles (24km) and a horizontal range of 28 miles (45km). The warhead is proximity fused or command-detonated, although the V750Vs and V750VKs used by the Ground Forces carry conventional warheads. The V75SM system is transportable, but it is not fired from a mobile launcher. The launcher is towed separately from the missile and is emplaced. The missile is then brought in on a trailer towed by an ATS-59-V, ZIL-157V or GT-TV tractor. Support equipment is similarly mobile. ECM development over the past decade has seriously degraded the effectiveness of the SA-2 system. In the later stages of the Vietnam War, the North Vietnamese Army was expending well over 80 missiles for every hit. In fact, the sight of SA-2s became so commonplace that they became known as 'Flying Telephone Poles'. Similarly, the Israeli Air Force, after experience of them in both 1967 and 1973, does not consider the threat of the SA-2 to be as serious as newer types such as the SA-6.

The smaller SA-3 Goa has supplemented the SA-2 in the low-altitude role since 1964. Goa is intended to cover the area, from about 110yds (100m) to 5,475yds (5,000m), where the SA-2 is less effective. It is a two-stage solid fuel missile using command/homing guidance in conjunction with the Low Blow radar operating in the 8.9-9.6 GHz band. It has a maximum vertical range of 7 miles (12km) and a horizontal range of 4-14 miles (6-22km). Goa, like the SA-2, is not fired from a mobile launcher, although the entire network is transportable. The launcher usually mounts two missiles, but a newer model carrying four missiles has been introduced. ECM techniques have also lessened the threat posed by the SA-3.

The SA-4 Ganef

The first fully mobile surface-to-air missile system was the SA-4 Ganef, which was introduced in 1964. Ganef is roughly comparable to the British Bloodhound and is powered by a solid fuel ramjet with four solid fuel boosters. It is carried on a fully-tracked lightly armoured chassis related to that now used by the SAU-152. Two missiles are carried on the launch vehicle, and the whole unit is air transportable aboard the AN-22 Antei. Ganef uses a command/homing guidance system with semi-active radar homing aerials in the fins in conjunction with the Pat Hand H-band target and tracking radar, which operates in the 6.44-6.68 GHz frequency range. In common with the other SA-2 and SA-3 guidance systems, the primary radar unit can be linked with the long-range Long Track E-band surveillance radar. The SA-4 has an effective vertical ceiling of 15 miles (24km) and a slant range of 43 miles (70km). It has never been encountered in combat and so its susceptibility to modern ECM techniques is less clear than in the case of the SA-2 and SA-3. Each Soviet Combined Arms Army usually fields a brigade of 9 batteries of SA-4,

each with 3 launchers, for a total of 27 launchers. In 1974, a new version, designated Ganef Mod 1 by NATO, made its first public appearance. It has a section of about 24in (60cm) round, a nose section with continuous taper and an improved launcher. It has improved low-altitude performance and is serving with Soviet and East German troops.

The SA-6 Gainful

In 1967, the Soviet Ground Forces began receiving a new generation of anti-aircraft weapons, the most effective of which was the SA-6 Gainful. Gainful is a sophisticated integrated ramjet-rocket powered missile. Three Gainful are carried on each tracked launch vehicle, which is a derivative of the prolific PT-76/GT family, and is very similar to the ZSU-23-4 chassis. Gainful has a vertical ceiling of 6 miles (10km) and slant range of 22 miles (35km).

However, it was Gainful's guidance system that really stood Western Intelligence on its ear. The Gainful utilizes semi-active homing, which homes in on reflected RF energy from continuous wave illumination in the Straight Flush radar. The older SA-2 and SA-3 used the more primitive monopulse techniques, track-while-scan methods and conical scanning. The SA-6 Gainful system is very similar to that used on the American Hawk, but its effectiveness was totally unexpected. The Straight Flush radar unit is as mobile as the missile launcher itself and is carried on the same basic chassis type. It operates in the 7.85-8.01 GHz frequency. The radar vehicle has an enormous radar array above the hull consisting of a target acquisition radar and a combination target tracking-target illumination radar. The unit probably carries 'identification friend or foe' (IFF) equipment.

Left: This overhead shot of a passing SA-6 shows the air intakes for the integrated rocket/ramjet engine. These intakes open up once the rocket engine has propelled the missile to a certain speed. (US Army)

Right: The SA-9 Gaskin appears to be a longer range and heavier version of the shoulder launched SA-7 Grail. It is mounted on a BRDM-2M chassis and is fully amphibious. The operator sits behind the glass window at the base of the launcher. When in transit or out of action, the entire launch array can be folded down onto the rear of the vehicle. (Sovfoto)

Bottom·right: The SA-8 Gecko is the newest and most sophisticated weapon of the PVO-SV. It appears to be based on a modified ZIL-167E truck chassis and normally carries four missiles. It has stowage capacity for at least another two reloads. The large central radar dish is the main tracking radar and the two smaller dishes to either side are probably used to gather the missiles very quickly when the system is being used against low-altitude targets. The vehicle is fully amphibious and has excellent cross-country abilities. (Sovfoto)

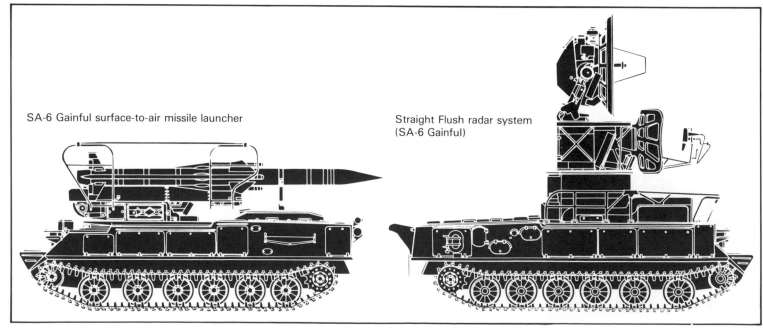

SA-6 Gainful surface-to-air missile launcher

Straight Flush radar system (SA-6 Gainful)

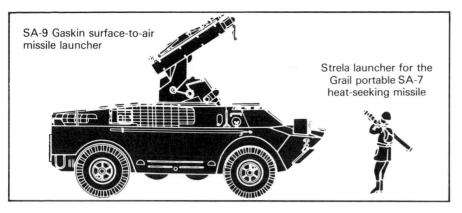

SA-9 Gaskin surface-to-air missile launcher

Strela launcher for the Grail portable SA-7 heat-seeking missile

The target illumination radar at the top of the assembly is a circular cassegrain type with full traverse independent of the lower acquisition radar. This radar operates in the 7.85-8.01 GHz range. The unit's microwave transmitter and receiver are housed in containers immediately behind the parabolic dish.

The Gainful missile itself is quite advanced, and its integrated ramjet-rocket propulsion system obviates the need for a separate booster, and thereby reduces the missile's overall size and weight by about a third. The missile uses rocket propulsion until a critical speed is reached, at which point air intakes are opened and the chamber is converted into a very efficient ramjet. This integrated propulsion system provides both efficient use of the fuel and excellent range. The warhead, which is a high explosive fragmentation type weighing about 176lb (80kg), is proximity fused and located behind a radome with a semi-active search radar.

The first public display of a complete Gainful system with the Straight Flush radar unit was at Oubeid in Egypt in 1974, though the weapon had been used in the October War of the previous year.

During the 1973 war, the Israelis relied heavily on American ECM techniques developed in Vietnam, but since the 1973 war was the first in which the Gainful was encountered, there was no practical experience in jamming its radar unit. Countermeasures had to be hastily developed to overcome the system, and suppression of SA-6 batteries proved to be among the most costly air missions of the war. Several tactical countermeasures were developed, and these lessened the casualties somewhat. Painful experience taught the Israelis that the Straight Flush's search capacity and altitude discrimination functions were limited and that, when aircraft were engaged in very steep dives, there were temporary blind spots. Some aircraft would attack in a steep dive while others maintained their distance and executed conventional ECM manoeuvres with electronic jamming and chaff. The effectiveness of this manoeuvre was heightened due to the fact that the missile's initial trajectory is somewhat low.

Another technique was to bring the aircraft in very low and confuse the radar by taking advantage of the ground clutter. The problem with both these techniques was that in concentrating on the SA-6, the pilots often left themselves exposed to accompanying Shilkas. Aircraft that escaped both were often set upon by SA-7 Grail portable heat-seeking missiles. About 40 per cent of Israeli Air Force losses were due to the SA-6.

This provides an excellent example of modern Soviet air defence. The attacker is forced to run a gauntlet of very different, intermixed defence systems. While any one system has its weaknesses, in trying to exploit one weakness, the attacker leaves himself exposed to the other supporting systems. In the European setting, the situation would be even worse since there are far more models available to the Warsaw Pact, and many of these are new types never encountered in combat.

The SA 9 Gaskin

Besides the portable SA-7, a related type using a larger engine, the SA-9 Gaskin, is now in service. This weapon is mounted on a modified BRDM-2, and four launchers are fitted onto a traversable, folding launch array. The larger engine and warhead of this weapon make it a more serious threat to opposing strike aircraft. There are sixteen of these vehicles per armoured division and per motorized rifle division.

The SA-8 Gecko

As surprising as the arrival of the SA-6 proved to be, the new SA-8 Gecko was even more of a shock. The SA-8 Gecko appears to be a direct counterpart to the Franco-German Roland system, and provides Soviet mobile forces with an all-weather, all-terrain, ECM resistant missile to fill the gap between the highly effective SA-6 and the SA-9 ZSU-23-4 Shilka combination. It seems to use a very sophisticated frequency hopping monopulse system that allows the Gecko launcher to salvo two missiles on different frequencies, thereby severely complicating ECM countermeasures. The SA-8 is mounted on a new six-wheeled amphibious all-terrain vehicle that is large enough to fit the missile launcher and radar assembly on

one mount. The new Land Roll radar operates in the 14.2-14.6 GHz frequency range and provides continuous early warning air surveillance, target tracking and missile tracking using a combination of radar and possibly low-light level television. The early warning radar seems to operate in the H-band at 4-8 GHz. The large tubular device above the tracking radar appears to be a telescope and camera for the low-light level television for operations during ECM jamming. The main target tracking radar uses the large parabolic cassegrain reflector in the centre of the main array, and is flanked by two smaller parabolic antennae used to provide missile-tracking information.

The new SA-8 provides an even denser concentration of fire in an already crowded tactical scene. The dense clutter of radar guidance systems has led NATO to assign priority to ECM jamming efforts, on the basis of the most serious threat. First priority goes to the jamming of the Straight Flush of the SA-6, followed by the Land Roll (SA-8), Gun Dish (ZSU-23-4), Flap Wheel (S-60 57mm gun), Pat Hand (SA-4), Low Blow (SA-3), Fan Song (SA-2) and Strategic Square Pair (for the SA-5, which is unlikely to be encountered).

The air defence complement of a typical Warsaw Pact Combined Arms Army is formidable. It provides a tightly interwoven defence of considerable mobility and firepower that, due to the wide variety of equipment and supporting radars, is reasonably resistant to ECM jamming.

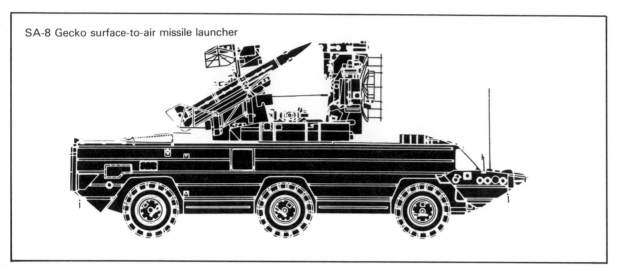

SA-8 Gecko surface-to-air missile launcher

MOBILE ANTI-AIRCRAFT MISSILE LAUNCHERS

US designation:	SA-4	SA-6	SA-8	SA-9
NATO designation:	Ganef	Gainful	Gecko	Gaskin
Chassis:	new	mod. PT-76	ZIL-167E4	BRDM-2
Crew:	3	3	4	3
Length:	31ft (9.6m)	24ft (7.3m)	30ft (9.1m)	18ft (5.4m)
Width:	10ft (3.2m)	10ft (3.2m)	9.5ft (2.9m)	7ft (2.1m)
Height:	17ft (5.2m)	11ft (3.3m)	13.5ft (4.1m)	9.5ft (2.9m)
Missiles deployed on launcher:	2	3	4	4
Additional stowed rounds:	0	0	0	4?
Missile length:	30ft (9.2m)	20ft (6.2m)	10ft (3.2m)	6ft (1.7m)
Fuselage diameter:	26ft (8.0m)	11ft (3.3m)	6ft (2.0m)	4ft (1.1m)
Weight:	40lbs (18.05kg)	12lbs (5.5kg)	4lbs (1.9kg)	7lbs (3.0kg)
Propulsion:	Solid booster liquid ramjet	Solid booster liquid ramjet	Solid fuel rocket	Solid fuel rocket
Guidance:	command/ homing	semi-active homing	command	passive IR
Horizontal range:	43 miles (70km)	22 miles (35km)	12 miles (20km)	4 miles (7km)
Vertical range:	15 miles (24km)	6 miles (10km)	7 miles (12km)	3 miles (4.5km)
Early Warning, Acquisition Radar, HF Radar:	Long Track, Thin Skin B	Long Track, Thin Skin B	Long Track, Thin Skin B	
Fire control radar:	Pat Hand	Straight Flush	Land Roll	
Operating frequency (GHz):	6.44-6.68	7.85-8.01	14.2-14.8	